Holy Qur

ISLAM

An Overview of its Ideology

Mujeeb Aslam Khan

© Copyright 2008 by Mujeeb Aslam Khan

Published by:	MAK - Quality Management Consultancy (UK)
Printed & bound by:	Think Ink Ltd, Ipswich, Suffolk IP2 8BH
Issue:	First Print - November 2008 Second Print - June 2010 (Additional information included)
ISBN-10:	0956079105
ISBN-13:	9780956079107
Recommended Price:	£4.95

A catalogue record for this book is available from the British Library

British Library's catalogue system No. 014870468

British National Bibliography (BNB) No. GBA905323

Cover pages designed and typeset by MAK

This book can be purchased from the Amazon.co.uk, WH Smith.co.uk, Foyles.co.uk and Waterstones.com web sites and their high street bookstores. In addition, copies are available at the major UK's public libraries and various Islamic bookshops in London for learned readers and multicultutral communities.

Note: Some of the quotations included in this book are in Arabic and taken directly from the holy Quran for reference, it is, therefore, requested that the text is handled with utmost respect and care. Thank you for your anticipated co-operation.

What the readers say....

"I am deeply honored to write the introduction to this book, which is a succinct and relevant aid for anyone who desires to be prepared for informed interaction with the ever-growing Muslim world." Professor Dr Akbar Ahmed - American University, Washington DC

"Th aim of the book is to present factual and essential material in a clear and concise style. This it has done. It is easy to read and does not get stalled in details while imparting the salient facts about Islam." Amanda Pigot, AB Publishing Services, Cambridge - UK

"This book is a quick and easily understood introduction to the basic beliefs of Islam, it seems to work very well, which is why it sits comfortably alongside the more academic books that already exist." Martin Howell, Libraries Stock Manager, Essex County Council - UK

"Congratulations on producing your excellent book on this very topical and prescient subject..." Chris Desmond, Reader Development Manager, East Sussex County Council - UK

"The scope and clarity of this book presents a brief and useful summary of Islam and its ethics." Ann Copus, Harrow Borough Council - UK

"This book is a timely publication and provides wealth of knowledge for multicultural communities, and all those who wish to know more about Islam and its followers." Manny Manoharan, Support and Development Manager, Waltham Forest Borough Council London - UK

"I can say without hesitation and with full confidence that, 'Islam: An overview of its ideology' written by Mujeeb Aslam Khan is an abridged encyclopaedia of Islam, its theology and jurisprudence. The author has compiled extremely useful and relevant information in his book, and he has conveyed the true message of Islam and tried to eradicate misunderstandings and misconceptions perceived in the West about Islam." Saqib Muneer Khan (R) Accountant and Writer - England

Dedication

As a humble servant
of God and student of Islam,
I dedicate this book to the one and only
Almighty God (Allah).

AND

To my late mother,
who was very kind, loving and
extremely caring; her unconditional
love and prayers have been inspiring
for me and my family.

Contents

Muslim population in the world

Demographic status of Islam and other major religions,
and projected growth rate between 2010 and 2050

Author's 5R Messages

Foreword

by

Professor Dr Akbar Ahmed

With 1.4 billion Muslims living worldwide and 57 Muslim nations, an understanding of Islam is crucial for every member of our global society. *Islam: An Overview of its Ideology* by Mujeeb Aslam Khan summarizes the key tenets of the fastest growing religion in the world. I am deeply honored to write the introduction to this book, which is a succinct and relevant aid for anyone who desires to be prepared for informed interaction with the ever-growing Muslim world.

The message that Khan presents in this book is not solely one of Islam, it is one of peace and tolerance. In our rapidly changing society, animosity and misunderstanding between religions is on the forefront of many of the world's conflicts. Such ethnic and religious bloodshed is both a cause and a result of the anger and ignorance of societies in the current age of globalization. Unfortunately, inter-religious and inter-cultural toleration continue to be undervalued.

There is a lack of knowledge about Islam by both Muslims and non-Muslims alike that cannot be ignored. The need to understand Islam reaches beyond the classrooms of our universities and into our homes, businesses and offices. An intricate understanding of this important world religion has never been of more political, cultural and social importance.

I am encouraged to see the promotion of interest in this subject by scholars such as Mujeeb Aslam Khan. By presenting information about the history and tenets of Islam in an accessible way, Khan is opening up the world of Islam to people of every level of education and experience. This book addresses Muslims as well as non-Muslims, as it discusses issues relevant to both groups. Khan diplomatically confronts key issues within Islam, such as the abundance of misperceptions from within and without, and how such misperceptions can be remedied.

The means of ensuring that we as an international community overcome the confrontations between our faiths is through dialogue and understanding. This book is certainly a step in the right direction. As someone actively involved in interfaith dialogue, I am very concerned with the need for understanding and compassion in this tumultuous time. And as a professor on the campus of American University, I am in a unique position to witness the power of dialogue within the classroom and observe how it can change perspectives. Mr. Khan's book brings the classroom to the world, allowing readers to enrich their own knowledge about Muslim society and enabling them to engage in the sort of bridge-building between cultures that is so essential in today's globalizing world.

Knowledge of the history and culture of the Muslim world is crucial for a deeper understanding of the inner workings of today's political society. I encourage the use of this book in living rooms, offices and classrooms alike to promote an informed discussion of the ever-growing world of Islam. I would like to thank Mujeeb Aslam Khan for his contributions to the development of this important subject.

Ambassador Akbar Ahmed
Ibn Khaldun Chair of Islamic Studies
American University
Washington, D.C.

Professor Dr Akbar Ahmed is the Ibn Khaldun Chair of Islamic Studies at American University. He is considered "the world's leading authority on contemporary Islam," according to the BBC. He is former High Commissioner of Pakistan to Great Britain, and has advised Prince Charles and met with President George W. Bush on Islam. His numerous books, films and documentaries have won prestigious awards and his books have been translated into several languages including Chinese and Indonesian. Dr Ahmed's most recent book, *Journey into Islam: The Crisis of Globalization*, is published by the Brookings Institution Press US.

This book presents much-needed authentic and impartial text in a clear, concise and coherent style for both Muslims and non-Muslims alike, and methodically covers Islamic ethics, important religious and social issues in an accessible way.

Preface

Like many devout Muslims, I also read the Quran to comprehend its ethics and obligatory duties as expected from all adherents. I always had a strong desire to enhance my knowledge and conduct an in-depth study of the Islamic ideology. In order to pursue my quest, I initially started my search in early 2005 to find a short book that could highlight major religious and social issues including a summary of the Quran's messages, an overview of each surah and correlation between the real life issues and Quran, etc. After a long search, my pursuit for such a text proved inconclusive. Because of this setback, a few ideas conceived in my mind, which inspired me to carry out my own thorough study of the Quran, and encouraged me to write a factual book about Islam for diverse communities. During my search, I came across many Islamic books written by several learned authors broadly covering different subjects and presented in traditional styles, mainly addressing Muslim readers.

My prime reason for writing this book is to fill the gap that existed, providing authentic and impartial text for both Muslims and non-Muslims alike compiled in a short book. Presenting the essence of the Quran for all those people who have been unable to read the holy book with meanings for deeper understanding, and clarifying unjust religious, scientific and social misconceptions about Islam.

In addition, my contribution will help to create more awareness and a better understanding of Islam. This book also outlines some of the major factors that initiate misperceptions, resentment and instigate unfair anti-Muslim propaganda in the world. As a result, some people are dejected and try to keep away from their religious and moral duties. Furthermore, it will encourage believers to conduct their own study of the Quran and Sunnah to understand the main messages, and its teachings will help to sustain enduring peace and harmony among the many different religions and beliefs.

I have no hesitation in stating that this book could not have been written without the blessing of Almighty God (Allah) and the prayers of my late mother. I feel privileged and grateful to have an opportunity to share my refined knowledge of Islam through my extensive study and research relating to Islamic ideology. I hope that learned readers will find the contents of this book informative and thought provoking and that the details presented will be used as cross-reference notes to improve their own knowledge of Islam. The text will also help to dispel the unjust myths and conspiracy theories about Muslims being portrayed in the media, which create a negative image of Islam and incites animosity around the world.

After accomplishing my writing task, I wanted a prominent author and leading scholar of Islam to review and write an introduction. In this regard, Professor Dr Akbar Ahmed was my first choice, because he is an intellectual and renowned writer, a well-respected speaker on international relations and a proactive advocate of Islamic teachings. Professor Ahmed very kindly acknowledged my request to write the foreword of my book, and I truly appreciated his support. I am delighted to have his valuable views on the subject.

As a student of Islam, I dedicate all my efforts and contribution to Allah (SWT) for promoting true Islamic messages and teachings without any personal or financial motives. I strongly believe that it is the duty of all Muslims to contribute and share their knowledge and good experience with other multicultural communities. Allah (SWT) will reward all those people who are sincere and endorse his messages of love, peace, tolerance and equality to avoid clash of ideologies among diverse religions and cultures, as Islam represents all humanity and promotes justice, mutual respect and harmony.

I hope that my contribution will encourage more interaction, better understanding and social cohesion among all faiths and cultures.

Mujeeb Aslam Khan

This book presents an abridged encyclopaedia and incisive guide to Islam, and will stand out as the most concise, authentic, timely and reliable introduction available after the 9/11 and 7/7 incidents.

In the name of Allah, the Most Gracious, the Most Merciful

1
Introduction

Naturally, when a child is born, his or her faith is pre-determined by inheriting two precious things from their parents: their genetic and religious identity for life. This means that immediately after birth the child is labelled as being born Muslim, Christian, Jew, Buddhist, Hindu, Sikh or Atheist, and does not have any choice to challenge or alter their birth identity. The newborn will certainly follow and benefit from their parents' cultural and religious beliefs until he or she is grown-up and able to make their own mind. In most cases, children observe everything their parents do and try to copy them; memories of their early life, upbringing and how the religious duties are fulfilled stay with them for the rest of their lives and are often passed on to their own children. For centuries, birth identity, religious and family values are transferred from one generation to another and this is a customary practice, which is followed by the many different beliefs and cultures of the world.

Religion is one of the leading topics, which most people regard as a private matter and, as a result, they are reluctant to discuss or express their views in public. Equally, many people are sceptical about their faith and think that religion is one of the major causes of current global conflicts. The question is why so many people are disheartened and support such phenomenon, and keep away from their religion or personal belief. Is it because of ignorance, lack of interest, disillusions and scepticism about diverse faiths, which distract some people to follow their religious obligations? Interfaith dialogue is one way to combat such doubts and misconceptions.

Living abroad amongst well cultured, learned and technologically developed communities and strictly following all guidelines mentioned in the Quran and Sunnah (Hadith) is a mammoth task for the majority of the believers of Islam. In reality, and mostly because of limited time and personal commitments, studying and thoroughly understanding the messages of the Quran and ethics of Islam are often overlooked or ignored. It is, therefore, not fully understood, misinterpreted and is regrettably being followed in a fragmented manner, as a modern lifestyle prevents many followers from their obligatory duties and conducting further study. This is one of the main problems, which initiate ignorance about Islam.

I am interested in reading articles and books that present Islamic ideology with facts, written in a concise and simple style. In the quest for such material, I initially visited many bookshops in London and surrounding areas, looking particularly for a book that could provide me with information relating to the core mandatory duties that Allah (SWT) conveyed to humanity through the holy book of Quran. I also wanted to use such a book for quick reference notes that could highlight the essence of the Quran, present a summary of each surah and cover issues relating to our daily life. For example, where in the Quran Allah (SWT) mentions the creation of universe and human beings; jihad; hajab/veil; women's role in Islam; and life after death, etc, etc. Obviously, in order to find out about any topic, one has to read the entire Quran and search for the surah that deals with the relevant topic. The process of correlating life issues with authentic Islamic teachings and text is time consuming and prevents many Muslims reading the Quran with meaning and following its messages.

Although I came across many books covering numerous issues in different styles and written by well-known learned authors, I could not find a short book covering major issues, which cross-references them with the relevant surah/chapter or ayah. In the end, I postponed my search and decided to conduct my own thorough study of the Quran. After over two years' extensive study and analysis of each surah/ayah, I made relevant notes that certainly enhanced my knowledge of the Quran and its teachings. Because of my in-depth study and analysis, I gained much greater understanding of Islam and its principles, and subsequently my refined knowledge enabled me to write and compile this unique and factual guidebook for multicultural communities.

After completing my in-depth study of the Quran in early 2007, I decided to put my views on paper and share my knowledge with my family and friends. After a few weeks, I fulfilled my primary objective and prepared a number of articles briefly covering most of the topics listed in this book. My initial intention was to publish the articles in the UK's newspapers for general awareness and to highlight constructive attributes of Islam, but after the death of my mother, I decided to write this book and devote all my efforts and contribution to Allah (SWT) for promoting love, peace, mutual respect and tolerance without any personal or financial motives.

In this book, I present a devout Muslim's perspective and the essence of Islam through authentic scriptures. I also want to clarify a number of misconceptions about Islam and how its followers are portrayed in the media, as these myths and conspiracy theories create Islamic phobia in some people's minds and initiate anti-Muslim propaganda and antipathy. This book also identifies some of the causes, which initiate animosity, distrust, doubts about Islam and clash of ideologies amongst nonbelievers and diverse faiths.

In order to know the basic ethics and attributes of Islam, it is essential that all Muslims first thoroughly read the Quran in Arabic and their native language, fully understanding its meanings, and, more importantly, sincerely follow and practice its teachings. Followers of Islam must also make extra efforts and read the authentic hadiths (sayings of the last Prophet Muhammad (pbuh) to broaden their knowledge of Islam, in the way Prophet Muhammad (pbuh) followed and preached the Quran's messages and teachings during his lifetime. This will take believers well beyond traditional and cultural teachings, enhance their personal knowledge, and will enable them to understand and practice their obligatory duties more flexibly and freely without any influence or fear.

In addition, this reference book will guide and help to improve the readers' knowledge about Islam, as it covers the important religious and social issues in a factual, clear and concise style. This book:

- presents an abridged encyclopaedia of Islam for both Muslims and non-Muslims alike, and includes a brief history, ethics and pillars of Islam, and essence of the Quran in a simple way
- provides a summary of the Quran for those people who have been unable to read the holy book with meaning
- highlights a correlation between the Quran and the vital life issues, and includes over 400 important quotes and relevant verses that prohibits killing of innocent people and terrorism
- identifies major factors that initiate animosity, distrust and clash of ideologies, and suggest what can be done to diffuse anti-Muslim propaganda, conspiracy theories and radicalism
- outlines common misconceptions about Islam and presents Muslims' perspective to clarify unjust delusions
- will help to promote the true messages of Islam and clarify the religious and social myths about Islam and 'Muslim-phobia' being unfairly conceived in some people's minds
- will facilitate readers to analyse religious, social and cultural differences, and how interfaith dialogue and bilateral efforts can help to bring diverse communities close to each other
- will help to create more awareness, and initiate theological debates about Islam after the 9/11 and 7/7 incidents
- will assist readers to conduct further study of the Quran, and will encourage more interaction with multicultural societies through love, peace, religious tolerance and social cohesion.

> Islam is for all humanity, and all human beings
> are equal and accountable to one and only creator
> Almighty God (Allah) regardless of their religion or race,
> and their good and bad deeds will be reviewed on the
> 'Judgment Day'. (Ref: Al Quran).

2

A brief history of Islam

The Quran is a holy book and guidance for Muslims and covers a variety of issues, including ethics and religious obligations. The word Islam simply means '<u>submission</u>' and is derived from the word 'Salama', meaning peace. In religious context it means '<u>total obedience to the will of God</u>'. In Arabic, Islam is called '<u>Deen</u>' (a way of life), and extensively followed all over the world.

Islam is not named after a tribe, people or an individual, as Judaism is named after the tribe Judah, Christianity after Christ and Buddhism after Buddha, etc. Islam is not a name chosen by a human being; it was communicated from Allah (SWT). Some people believe that Islam started with Prophet Muhammad (pbph), but according to the Quran and Islamic teachings it was Adam who first brought Islam to human race. After Adam, Allah (SWT) sent over 124,000 messengers and all prophets tried their utmost during their lifetime to successfully convey and preach Allah's messages and commandments to their respective people, until Allah (SWT) chose and sent the last Prophet Muhammad (pbuh) to spread Islam through the revelation of the Quran for humanity.

It is undoubtedly a total belief of every Muslim and adherents that the holy book of Quran was revealed in stages to the last and final Prophet Muhammad (pbuh) over 1400 years ago in Mecca and Madina (Saudi Arabia), and its words are true, original, unchanged and will not be altered or misquoted at any time. The Quran was revealed when non-believers dominated the Arab world during 600 CE and created difficulties for those people who believed in the one and only ultimate creator of all things - Almighty God. After 23 years of its revelation under the guidance and leadership of the last and final Prophet Muhammad (pbuh) Islam flourished and became the dominant religion in the Arab world, and today Islam is the fastest growing religion in the US, UK, Europe and Africa.

Islam is spreading rapidly and currently is the second largest and most popular religion after Christianity. There are about 1.5 billion Muslims representing between 21 and 23% of the total world population in 57 Muslim nations who follow the Quran's messages and Islamic ethics within their respective cultures and countries.

The question is why after over 600 years later, when Christianity was well established, Islam emerged as a dominant religion and persuaded non-believers to accept that there is only one Almighty Allah (God) who created all human beings, creatures and the universe and that there is no other person (dead or alive) or spiritual power worthy of worshipping. The answers to these and other questions are explained in the Quran and revolve around its teachings, ethics, basic beliefs and five pillars of Islam. This means a total faith that there is only one ultimate creator, Allah (SWT), worthy of worshipping in all circumstances and difficulties. Praying five times a day during dawn and late evening, giving Zakat (i.e. helping poor people - It is obligatory for all Muslims to give 2.5% of their earnings and savings every year), fasting during the month of Ramadan, and finally performing Hajj pilgrimage to Mecca once in a lifetime. In addition, all Muslims are required to study and observe other important guidelines, as explained in the Quran and authentic hadiths. This is the essence of Islam and in-depth study will help Muslims to understand its main messages and apply them more flexibly without any influence.

Islam is a peaceful religion and promotes love, peace, tolerance, mutual respect, integrity and kindness to humanity. Islam also encourages acquiring and sharing knowledge, equality and justice for all civilization without any compulsion or discrimination.

In Surah Al - Maidah C 5: V3 Allah (SWT) says that:

"...This day have I perfected your religion for you and completed my favour unto you and have chosen for you a religion AL - ISLAM..."

3
Major attributes of God (Allah)

Al Quran - Surah Al Baqara - C2: V163 - *"And your God is One God; there is no God but He, Most Gracious, Most Merciful."*

Surah An-Nisa C4: V48 - *"Surely Allah will not forgive the associations with Him, but forgives whomever He wishes..."*

Surah Al Anaam - C6: V102 - *"That is Allah your Lord! There is no God but He, the creator of all things: then worship Him: and He hath power to dispose of all affairs."*

Surah Al-Anaam C6: V162 - *Say; "Truly my prayer, my sacrifice, my life and death are for Allah, Lord of the Worlds"*

Surah Ash-Shura C42: V11 - *"...There is nothing like Him (Allah) and He sees and hears all things"*

Allah is an Arabic word meaning 'The One and only true Deity' who created universe, human beings, heaven and the earth. Jews and Christians call him their 'God.' All Muslims believe that there are unknown attributes of Allah (SWT) to imagine, think or list, as he is the greatest, the most merciful and there is no other than him worthy of praying to and worshipping. Muslims regard themselves lucky and grateful to Allah (SWT) for his kindness, mercy and allowing them to be his followers. Some of Allah's qualities are mentioned in the Surah Hadid C57: V 1 - 29 that includes the following major attributes and special powers of Allah (SWT):

- Allah-o-Akbar - Allah is the greatest. There is no other person (deceased/alive) or spiritual power worth worshipping or praying to. There is only one Almighty God (Allah).

- Allah (SWT) created the universe, all human beings, angels, animals, and nobody created him. He does not have a father, mother or son. He is a supreme power and controls all the activities of angels, the universe, Jinn's and human beings.

- Allah (SWT) has the ultimate power and knows everything (our past and future actions/deeds), time of birth, death, provides us with health, wealth and controls our destiny, and he knows the time of the final judgment day and when it will happen.

- Whatever Allah (SWT) intends to do just happen and nothing happens without his intention or will. An unknown number of angels pray and follow Allah's instructions day and night as part of their obligatory duty and obedience.

- Allah (SWT) likes and helps those people who are honest and have sincere intentions, follow the guidelines mentioned in the Quran and Hadith and are kind to all other human beings.

- Allah (SWT) dislikes all those people who create Allah's Shareeks/associates (pray and worship to other than Allah), visit mizars for help (dead people's graves for spiritual support), pray and ask deceased people to help them, and children who are disobedient to their parents and do not look after them.

- Allah (SWT) listens to all prayers and answers them accordingly (what is best for us), providing that prayers and intentions are sincere for individuals and other people.

- Allah (SWT) is the most gracious and kind and forgives whomever he wishes. Muslims must, therefore, sincerely worship him and be grateful for his kindness and mercy.

In Surah Al Baqara C 2: V152 Allah (SWT) states that:
"Remember me (by praying) and I will remember you, be grateful to me and never be ungrateful to me"

Also, in Surah Al Mumin C 40: V60 Allah (SWT) says that:
"Pray unto me and I will hear your prayer…"

4
Basic beliefs and pillars of Islam

A Muslim cannot be a Muslim until he or she sincerely accepts and practice the following obligatory beliefs and pillars of Islam, as stated in the Quran (Ref: C2: V177). This is the essence of Islam.

i) **Total belief in Allah (SWT)**
    All believers must truthfully accept that there is only one God (Allah SWT), who is the creator of all human beings, creatures and the entire universe. He does not have any son, father, mother or family. In the Surah Al Ikhlas - C112: V1 to V4 Allah's attributes are mentioned as - *Say, "He is God (Allah), the One and only, Allah, the Eternal, Absolute. He begetteth not, nor was He begotten, and there is none comparable unto Him."*

ii) **Belief in Angels**
    All Muslims believe in the existence of the angels and that they were created from light. There are an unknown number of angels; all worship Allah (SWT), obey him and act only by his command. Angels are the most obedient servants of Allah.

iii) **Belief in Allah's (SWT) revealed books**
    All Muslims believe that Allah (SWT) revealed four books to his messengers as a proof for humanity and guidance for them. The following books are mentioned in the Quran:

    • The original Torah revealed to Prophet Musa (pbuh).
    • The original Zabur sent to Prophet Daud (pbuh).
    • The original Injeel sent to Prophet Jesus (pbuh).
    • The Quran revealed to Prophet Muhammad (pbuh).

iv) **Belief in the Prophets and all Messengers of Allah (SWT)**
    All Muslims believe in the messengers of Allah (SWT), including Prophets Adam, Noah, Abraham, Ismail, Issac, Jacob, Moses and Jesus, etc. (peace be upon them all). Prophet Muhammad (pbuh) was the last prophet of Allah (SWT).

v) Belief in the Day of Judgment

All Muslims believe in the 'Day of Judgment', when all human beings will be resurrected for judgment and results according to their belief and deeds.

vi) Belief in Divine Decree (Predestination)

All Muslims believe that Allah (SWT) has full power and knowledge of all things happens on earth and other planets, and nothing happens without his command, and he knows everything about our past, present and future events.

Pillars of Islam

- **Shahada** - accepting that there is <u>one true deity</u> - God (Allah).
- **Salat** - praying <u>five times</u> a day (Fajar, Zohr, Isar, Mugrib, Isha).
- **Zakat** - annually giving <u>2.5%</u> of the personal wealth in charity .
- **Sawm** - fasting during the month of Ramadan is mandatory.
- **Hajj** - is an obligation once in a lifetime for all those Muslims who are physically and financially able to fulfil their duty.

The following diagram shows a link between the Quran and Islamic ideology.

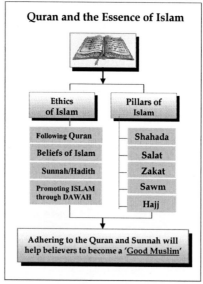

Drawn by - MAK

5
About Prophet Ibrahim (pbuh)

Prophet Ibrahim (pbuh) played a pivotal role in early Islamic history when unbelievers dominated the Arab world and there was no sign of Islam. He is also regarded as a founding father of the Abrahamic religions such as Judaism, Christianity and Islam. Prophet Ibrahim (Abraham) was born during 1950 BCE into a typical family of that ancient time (also known as Babylonia); his father (Azhar) was a musrik (unbeliever) who openly rejected the existence of Allah (SWT) and who made statues of their so-called gods and placed them in a local temple for worshipping.

During the early childhood, Prophet Ibrahim (pbuh) realized that his father made strange statues. One day he asked him about them and his father replied that he made statues of gods. Prophet Ibrahim (pbuh) was astonished and strongly rejected and refused to accept statues as being God. He told his father about the one and only Almighty God (Allah) and his existence. The difference of beliefs continued to exist between them, and after a few years Prophet Ibrahim (pbuh) decided to openly confront unbelievers and told them about the one and only Almighty Allah (SWT). He was determined to stamp out their practices, and went to a local town to discuss with the people and tried to persuade them about the one and only God.

Prophet Ibrahim (pbuh) explained that their ancestors had been wrongly worshipping idols. This angered unbelievers and they said, "Are you condemning our gods and forefathers?" Prophet Ibrahim (pbuh) showed no fear as he replied, "I am serious; I come to you with a true religion. I have been sent with guidance from our Lord (Allah), who alone is worthy of worshipping, who is the creator of the universe and human beings and controls our life and destiny, unlike the dumb idols, which are just made of clay, stone and wood and do nothing".

Prophet Ibrahim (pbuh) also asked unbelievers, "Do the idols see you when you worship them, and do they benefit you in any way?" They tried to defend their beliefs and argued that they knew the idols were lifeless, but their forefathers had worshipped them for years and these reasons were good enough for them to follow. In order to convince unbelievers that the idols could not harm him, Prophet Ibrahim (pbuh) challenged them by saying "I have already condemned them and if they had any power they would have harmed me by now." He continued to preach and performed various miracles to persuade unbelievers about the existence of the one and only Almighty Allah (SWT). Prophet Ibrahim (pbuh) experienced considerable hardship and unbelievers created many obstacles, which did not deter him, as his belief in Allah (SWT) and Islam consolidated and progressed further with total commitment, determination and passion.

Prophet Ibrahim (pbuh) later married Bibi Sarah and Bibi Hajira and had two sons, Ismail (pbuh) (from Bibi Hajira) and Issac (pbuh), (from Bibi Sarah). He later migrated to other areas of Arab land and preached Allah's (SWT) messages, encountered problems, and performed many miracles and successfully converted many unbelievers to Islam. His son Ismail (pbuh) also played an important role, as he obediently followed and supported his father's wish and total faith in Allah (SWT) and Islam. As a result of their sincere efforts, positive contributions, devotion and passion, Islam later flourished throughout the Arab world and subsequently other messengers of Allah (SWT) continued their mission and true teachings during their respective lifetimes with dedication, total commitment and without any influence or fear.

Prophet Ibrahim's (pbuh) contributions are well respected and he is regarded in Islam as being the 'founding father', as he and his son Ismail rebuilt the Kaaba in Mecca in difficult circumstances when unbelievers dominated the Middle East and refused to accept the existence of the one and only God. Prophet Ibrahim (pbuh) died during 1775 BCE at the age of 175 and left behind a legacy of Abrahamic faiths (i.e. Judaism, Christianity and Islam).

6
Salient features of the Quran

Holy Quran

Al-Quran Surah Yusuf C12: V2 - *"We have sent it down as an Arabic Qur'an, in order that ye may learn wisdom."*

The Quran comes from the root word Qara'a, which means 'to read' or 'to recite'. The word Quran therefore, means recitation. The Quran is the holy book for Muslims, revealed in Arabic for whole humanity and covers a variety of issues including the ethics, history, religious duties and guidance. Through the Quran, Islam teaches unity, tolerance, love for human beings, justice, fairness and respect for all faiths, etc. The Quran instructs Muslims to follow its messages and avoid evil things, which are forbidden in Islam.

In the following surahs, the attributes of the Quran are stated:

Surah Al Isra - C17: V88 - *Say: "If the whole of mankind and Jinns were to gather/unite together to produce the like of this Qur'an, they could not produce the like thereof, even if they backed up each other with help and support."*

Surah Al Isra - C17: V106 - *"(It is) a Qur'an which We have divided (into parts from time to time), in order that thou mayst recite it unto men at intervals: We have revealed it by (successive) revelation."*

Surah Fatir - C35: V29 - *"Those who rehearse/read the Book of Allah, establish regular prayer, and spend (in Charity) out of what we have provided for them, secretly and openly, hope for a commerce that will never fail."*

The following are some useful facts about the Quran:

- The Angel Gabriel (Jibrail) revealed the Quran to the last and final Prophet Muhammad (pbuh) in stages between 610 CE and 632 CE in Mecca and Madina, and was completed in 23 years.

- In 633 CE, Abu Bakr (pbuh) compiled the Quran into one volume, and later Umar Farooq and Usman (pbut) finalised the Quran.

- The Quran is the holy book in its original transcript without a single word altered or changed. It contains 114 surahs (chapters) and 6,236 ayats/verses (excluding Bismilas), which are collated in 30 parts/Juz and completes the Quran for Muslims. (86 surahs were revealed in Mecca and 28 were revealed in Madina).

- All surahs except one (Surah 9 At-Taubah) begin with the sentence *Bismillahir rahmanir raheem.* Surah Al Fatihah is the first and Surah An-Naas is the last surah of the Quran. Allah's (SWT) name is mentioned 2,698 times in the holy Quran.

- Surah Al Baqara is the longest, has 286 verses whereas Surah Al Kuser is one of the shortest, and contains only three verses. There are 99 different names of Allah (SWT) listed in the Quran, i.e. Ar Rehman, Ar Rhaeem, Al Kareem, Al Ghafur, Al Razak and Al Akeem etc. (Please also see Appendix 'A').

- All words of the Quran are original, true, have not been changed and will not be altered at any time. The Quran is a holy book for Muslims and must regularly be read/recited in Arabic (with translation/meanings in other native languages), and its messages must be fully understood and followed.

- Allah (SWT) has sent about 124,000 Prophets/Nabis, but only 25 prophets are mentioned in the Quran. The Quran has used both words, Nabi and Rasool. The difference between them is that a Rasool was a messenger of Allah who was given a new Shariat/Rasalut (revaluation/introduced a new religion) from Him, and a Nabi was also the messenger of Allah, but was not given any new Shariat and followed the faith of earlier Rasool.

- In the Quran, only five Rasools/messengers names are mentioned, i.e. Prophet Nuh, Ibrahim/Abraham, Musa/Moses, Issa /Jesus and Prophet Muhammad (peace be upon them all).

- According to the Quran, Adam (pbuh) was the first messenger of Allah (SWT) and Muhammad (pbuh) was the last and final prophet who introduced Islam at the age of 40 in Mecca.

- There are six surahs (chapters) in the Quran, which are named after prophets. These relevant surahs are: 1. Surah Yunus, 2. Surah Hud, 3. Surah Yusuf, 4. Surah Ibrahim, 5. Surah Nuh and 6. Surah Muhammad. Also Bibi Maryam (Mary) is the only woman mentioned by name in the Quran.

- Only four angels' names are mentioned in the Quran (ie. Angel Jibrail (pbuh), Angel Meekail (pbuh), Angels Haroot & Maroot). Surah YaSin (C36) is regarded as the heart of the Quran.

- Five mosques are mentioned in the Quran. These are: 1. Masjid-e-Haram in Mecca, 2. Masjid-e-Nabawwi in Madina, 3. Masjid-e-Aqsa in Baitul Muqaddas, Palestine, 4. Masjid-e-Quba in Madina, 5. Masjid-e-Zarar in Madina.

- In the Quran, the importance of the Salah and Zakat is mentioned over 700 and 150 times respectively.

- There are four different names of the Quran mentioned: Al-Furqaan, Al-Kitaab, Al-Zikr and Al-Huda.

- In the Quran, Allah (SWT) mentions a few prophets' disobedient tribes and nations, and how he destroyed them. For example, Prophet Noah's nation was destroyed by a severe storm (Ref: C71: V25), Prophet Lut's tribe was terminated by heavy rain and stones thrown from the sky (Ref: Al Quran C54: V33-V36), and Prophet Musa's people were turned into apes (Ref: C2: V65).

- In 1153, the Quran was translated into Latin, and later in 1649, Alexander Ross translated the Quran into English from French.

- The Quran recognises other Abrahamic faiths such as Judaism and Christianity including Prophet Jesus (pbuh), etc.

The following pages are compiled to help and enhance the knowledge of those people who have been unable to read the Quran with meanings. The important surahs listed below briefly highlight duties, obedience and the significance of life. In order to comprehend the messages conveyed by Allah (SWT) for all humanity, it is essential that the Quran is read with meanings and the issues mentioned within fully understood. It is imperative that all Muslims thoroughly read the Quran and follow its teachings.

Surah Al Fatihah C1: V1-V7 - *This surah is recited during the pray (Salah) which is obligatory for all Muslims. It states:*

"In the name of Allah, Most Gracious, Most Merciful. Praise be to Allah, Lord of the worlds; Most Gracious, Most Merciful; Owner of the Day of Judgment; Thee (alone) we worship; Thee (alone) we ask for help; Show us the straight way, Not (the path) of those who earn Thine anger nor of those who go astray."

Surah Baqara C2: V7 - *"Allah hath sealed their (unbelievers) hearing and hearts, and on their eyes there is a covering".*

Surah Baqara C2: V18 - *Unbelievers are "deaf, dumb and blind".*

Surah Baqara C2: V21 - *"O mankind! Worship your Lord, Who hath created you and those before you, so that ye may ward off (evil)."*

Surah Baqara C2: V23 - *"And if ye are in doubt concerning that which We reveal unto Our slave (Muhammad), then produce a surah of the like thereof, and call your witness beside Allah if ye are truthful."*

Surah Baqara C2: V43 - *"Establish Salah and pay Zakat"*

Surah Baqara C2: V98 - *"Who is an enemy to Allah, and His angels and His messengers, and Gabriel and Michael! Then, lo! Allah (Himself) is an enemy to the disbelievers."*

Surah Baqara C2: V115 - *"Unto Allah belong the East and the West, and wherever you turn, there is Allah's countenance and presence..."*

Surah Baqara C2: V127 - *In this surah about Kaaba is mentioned and it states that "And when Abraham and Ishmael were raising the foundations of the House, (Abraham prayed): Our Lord! Accept from us (this duty)..."*

Surah Baqara C2: V136 - *"Say (O Muslims): We believe in Allah and that which is revealed unto us and that which was revealed unto Abraham, and Ishmael, and Isaac, and Jacob, and the tribes, and that which Moses and Jesus received, and that which the prophets received from their Lord. We make no distinction between any of them..."*

Surah Baqara C2: V152 - *"Therefore remember Me, I will remember you. Be grateful to Me and never be ungrateful to Me."*

Surah Baqara C2: V168 - *"O mankind! Eat of that which is lawful and wholesome in the earth and follow not the footsteps of the devil as he is an open enemy for you." (This surah advices about halal and haram in Islam).*

Surah Baqara C2: V177 - *Qualities of a 'Good Muslim' stated in this surah together with beliefs and pillars of Islam as listed on pages 9 & 10.*

Surah Baqara C2: V183 - *"O ye who believe! Fasting is prescribed for you, even as it was prescribed for those before you..."*

Surah Baqara C2: V190 - *"Fight in the way of Allah against those who fight against you, but begin not hostilities..."*

Surah Baqara C2: V195 - *"Spend your wealth for the cause of Allah, and be not cast by your own hands to ruin; and do good..."*

Surah Baqara C2: V208 - *"O ye who believe! Come, all of you, into submission (unto Him); and follow not the footsteps of the devil..."*

Surah Baqara C2: V228 - *"...And they (women) have rights similar to those (of men) over them in kindness..."*

Surah Baqara C2: V245 - *"Who is it that will lend unto Allah a goodly loan, so that He may give it increase manifold..." (i.e. Zakat and charity).*

Surah Baqara C2: V256 - *"There is no compulsion in religion..."*

Surah Al Imran C3: V3 - *"He hath revealed unto thee (Muhammad) the Scripture with truth, confirming that which was (revealed) before it, even as He revealed the Torah and the Gospel (Bible)."*

Surah Al Imran C3: V12 - *"Say (O Muhammad) unto those who disbelieve: Ye shall be overcome and gathered unto Hell..."*

Surah Al Imran C3: V18 - *"Allah (Himself) is Witness that there is no God save Him. And the angels and the men are too witness..."*

Surah Al Imran C3: V31 - *"Say, (O Muhammad, to mankind): If ye love Allah, follow me; Allah will love you and forgive your sins..."*

Surah Al Imran C3: V95 - *"Say: Allah speaketh truth. So follow the religion of Abraham, the upright. He was not of the idolaters."*

Surah Al Imran C3: V103 - *"Hold tight to Allah's rope all together; do not split into factions..."* (This surah emphasises about Muslims unity).

Surah Al Imran C3: V132 - *"And obey Allah and the messenger (Muhammad – pbuh), that you may find mercy".*

Surah Al Imran C3: V145 - *"No soul can ever die except by Allah's leave and at a term appointed... We bestow on him thereof...."*

Surah Al Imran C3: V185 - *"Every soul will taste of death ..."*

Surah An Nisa C4: V1 - *"...your Lord who created you from a single soul and from it created its mates..."*

Surah An Nisa C4: V29 - *"...and do not kill yourselves (nor kill one another.) Surely Allah is Most merciful to you."*

Surah An Nisa C4: V34 - *"Men are in charge of women because Allah hath made the one of them to excel the other..."*

Surah An Nisa C4: V59 - *"O ye who believe! Obey Allah, and obey the messenger..."* (The last and final Prophet Muhammad (pbuh).

Surah Al Maidah C5:V3 - *"...chosen for you Islam as your religion..."*

Surah Al Maidah C5: V6 - *This surah explains how to perform Vuzoo.*

Surah Al Maidah C5: V32 - *"...whoever kills a human being for other than manslaughter or corruption in the earth, it shall be as he had killed all mankind, and likewise if anyone saves the life of one, it shall be as if he had saved the life of all mankind..."*

Surah Al Anaam C6: V1 - *"...Allah, Who hath created the heavens and earth and appointed darkness and light..."*

Surah Al Anaam C6: V2 - *"He it is Who hath created you from clay and hath decreed a term for you. A term is fixed with him..."*

Surah Al Anaam C6: V121 - *"And eat not of that whereon Allah's name hath not been mentioned..."* (This surah refers to halal & haram).

Surah Al Anaam C6: V151 - "... *that ye ascribe no thing as partner unto Him and that you do good to your parents, and that ye slay not your children because of penury (poverty) - We provide for you and for them*"

Surah Al Anaam C6: V160 - "... *Anybody bringeth a good deed will receive tenfold the like thereof, while whoso bringeth an ill-deed will be awarded but the like thereof; and they will not be wronged.*"

Surah Al Anaam C6: V162 - Say; "*Truly my prayer, my sacrifice, my life and death are for Allah, Lord of the Worlds*"

Surah Al Araf C7: V204 - "*And when the Quran is recited listen carefully and pay full attention...*"

Surah Al Anfal C8: V28 - "*And know that your possessions and your children are a test, and that Allah is immense reward.*"

Surah Al Anfal C8: V46 - "*And obey Allah and His Messenger, and fall into no disputes, lest ye lose heart and your power depart; and be patient and persevering: For Allah is with those who patiently persevere*"

Surah Tauba C9: V30 - "*And the Jews say: Ezra is the son of Allah, and the Christians say: The Messiah is the son of Allah. That is their saying with their mouths. They imitate the saying of those who disbelieved of old. Allah (Himself) fighteth against them...*"

Surah Tauba C9: V112 - "*(Triumphant) are those who turn repentant (to Allah), those who serve (Him), those who praise (Him), those who fast, those who bow down, those who fall prostrate (in worship), those who enjoin the right and who forbid the wrong and those who keep the limits (ordained) of Allah - And give glad tidings to believers!*"

Surah Yunus C10: V3 - "*Lo! your Lord is Allah Who created the heavens and the earth in six Days, then He established Himself upon the Throne, directing all things. There is no intercessor (with Him) save after His permission. That is Allah, your Lord, so worship Him...*"

Surah Yunus C10: V9 - "*Lo! those who believe and do good works, their Lord guideth them by their faith. Rivers will flow beneath them ...*"

Surah Yunus C10: V13 - "*We destroyed the generations before you when they did wrong; and their messengers (from Allah) came unto them with clear proofs (of His Sovereignty) but they would not believe...*"

Surah Yunus C10: V28 - *On the day when We gather them all together, then We say unto those who ascribed partners (unto Us): Stand back, ye and your (pretended) partners (of Allah)! And We separate them, the one from the other, and their partners say: It was not us ye worshipped."*

Surah Yunus C10: V65 - *"... Lo! power belongs wholly to Allah. He is the Hearer, the Knower." (This surah states that Allah is the Almighty).*

Surah Yunus C10: V89 - *"... Your prayer is heard. Do ye twain keep to the straight path, and follow not the road of those who have no knowledge."*

Surah Hud C11: V7 - *"And He it is Who created the heavens and earth in six days...Which of you is best in conduct ..."*

Surah Hud C11: V85 - *"Give full measure and weight in justice... And do not evil in the earth, causing corruption."*

Surah Ar Raad C13: V2 - *"Allah it is Who raised up the heavens without visible supports, then mounted the Throne, and compelled the sun and the moon to be of service, each runneth unto an appointed term; He ordereth the course; He detaileth the revelations, that haply ye may be certain of the meeting with your Lord."*

Surah Ar Raad C13: V26 - *"Allah enlargeth livelihood for whom He will, and straiteneth (it for whom He will); and they rejoice in the life of the world, whereas the life of the world is but brief comfort as compared with the Hereafter." This is a reminder that the life on eath is temporary.*

Surah Ar Raad C13: V8 - *"Allah knoweth that which every female beareth and that which the wombs absorb and that which they grow..."*

Surah Ar Raad C13: V9 - *" He is the Knower of the Invisible and the Visible, the Great, the High Exalted."*

Surah Ar Raad C13: V29 - *"Those who believe and do right: Joy is for them, and bliss (their) journey's end.*

Surah Al Hijr C15: V44 - *"The hell has seven gates..."*

Surah Al Isra (Bani Israil) C17: V78 - *"Establish worship (Salah) at the sunset until the dark, and recite of the Quran at dawn..."*

Surah An Noor C24: V26 - *"On the Day when their tongues, their hands, and their feet will bear witness against them as to their actions.*

Surah An Noor C24: V26 - "...*Good women are for good men and good men are for good women...*" *(Equally bad women are for bad men.)*

Surah Yaseen C36: V12 - "*Verily We shall give life to the dead, and We record that which they send before and that which they leave behind, and of all things have We taken account in a clear Book (of evidence).*"

Surah Yaseen C36: V32 - "*But each one of them all - will be brought before Us (for judgment).*" *This is the reminder about judgment day.*

Surah Yaseen C36: V65 - "*This day We seal up their mouths, and their hands speak out to Us and their feet bear witness as to what they did.*"

Surah Az-Zumar C39: V70 - "*And each soul is paid in full for what it did. And he is well aware of what they do.*"

Surah Ash-Shura C42: V50 - Allah "*provides whomever he wishes sons and daughters or both, and give no family whomever he wishes...*"

Surah Al Ahqaf C46: V15 - "*And we have commended unto man kindness towards parents...*" *(This surah advises about parents respect).*

Surah Al Hujurat C49: V6 - "*O ye who believe! If a wicked person comes to you with any news, ascertain the truth, lest ye harm people unwittingly and afterwards become full of repentance for what ye did.*"

Surah Al Hujurat C49: V10 - "*The Believers are but a single Brotherhood: So make peace and reconciliation between your two (contending) brothers; and fear Allah, that ye may receive Mercy.*"

Surah Al Hujurat C49: V12 - "*...And spy not, neither backbite one another. Would one of you love to eat the flesh of his dead bother...*"

Surah Al Hujurat C49: V15 - "*The true believers are those who only believe Allah and His messenger ...*" *(This is the essence of Islam).*

Surah Al Hujurat C49: V18 - "*Allah knows the secrets of the heavens and earth: He sees everything you do.*"

Surah Al Ikhlas C112: V1-V4 - *This surah is also recited during the obligatory pray (Salah) and restates that there is only one God (Allah), and he has no associates or family. He has the ultimate power of everything. C112: V1 "Say: He is Allah, the One and Only; C114: V2 - Allah, the Eternal, Absolute; C114: V3 - He begetteth not, nor was He begotten; C114: V4 - And there is none like unto Him".*

7
A brief life history of the Prophet Muhammad (pbuh)

مُحَمَّدٌ رَّسُولُ ٱللَّهِ

"Muhammad is the Messenger of Allah..." (Surah Al-Fath C48: V29)

لَاۤ إِلَهَ إِلَّا ٱللَّهُ مُحَمَّدٌ رَّسُولُ ٱللَّهِ

"La ilaha illa Allah, Muhammadur rasoolu Allah."

Meaning - "There is no true god (deity) but Allah, and Muhammad (pbuh) is the Rasool (Prophet, Nabi and Messenger) of Allah".

In Islamic history, Prophet Muhammad (pbuh) is regarded as a pioneer and last messenger; he played a pivotal role in conveying Allah's messages and in the process encountered many obstacles. However, his total faith and passion did not deter him and later Islam flourished throughout the Arab world. The following are some useful facts about last and final Prophet Muhammad (pbuh):

- Prophet Muhammad (pbuh) was born on 12 Rabi-al-Awwal - 570 CE in Mecca; his father Abdullah (pbuh) died before his birth and mother Bibi Amina (pbuh) passed away when he was about six years old. As a result, Prophet Muhammad (pbuh) was an orphan and illiterate (could not read or write Arabic).

- Prophet Muhammad (pbuh) was placed in the care of his grandfather Abdul-Muttalib (pbuh), and after 578 CE, his uncle Abu Talib (pbuh) looked after him and spent most of his early life in Mecca. His uncle Abu Talib was head of a Hashim clan and was a very influential man among his tribes.

- Prophet Muhammad (pbuh) married Bibi Khadija at the age of 25 and they had six children, two sons (Abd-Allah and Qasim; both died shortly after the birth) and four daughters (Bibi Ruqayyah, Bibi Umm Kulthum, Bibi Zainab and Bibi Fatimah).

- Bibi Fatimah was the most prominent and loving daughter, and holds a special and very high place in Islam. She married Hazrat Ali (pbuh) (Prophet Muhammad's cousin) and had two sons, Hussen (pbuh) and Hussain (pbuh), who later sacrificed their lives and entire family for the sake of Allah and protected Islam for humanity. All Mulsims are grateful for their sacrifice.

- Prophet Muhammad (pbuh) spent over twenty-four years preaching Allah's messages as listed in the holy book of Quran. The first surah was revealed during the month of Ramadan and the Quran was completed within 23 years.

- Angel Gabriel called upon and revealed Allah's messages to Prophet Muhammad (pbuh) during 610 CE, while he was praying in a cave on the Mount Hira outside Mecca.

- Prophet Muhammad (pbuh) migrated to Madina during 622 CE (in Islamic history, this period is known as Hijjarat meaning migration), and prophet stayed there until 632 CE.

- Prophet Muhammad (pbuh) and his followers fought various battles with unbelievers; Budder (624 CE), Udha (625 CE) and outside Mecca in 632 CE have been the most prominent and influential battles in Islamic history.

- Prophet Muhammad (pbuh) performed his pilgrimage (Hajj) during 632 CE and after a few months passed away in Madina at the age of 63. After his death the four Caliphs, (Abu Bakr, Umer, Othman (Usman) and Hazrat Ali (pbut-all) respectively continued the legacy and preached Islam with passion.

- A Muslim cannot be a Muslim who contradicts that Prophet Muhammad (pbuh) was the last and final messenger of Allah.

In the following surahs, Allah (SWT) states that:

"Say (O' Muhammad to mankind), if you love Allah, follow me; Allah will love you and forgive your sins..."
(Ref: Surah Al-Imran C3:V31)

"...Muhammad is the last prophet of Allah..." (Ref: C33: V40)

8
Qualities of a 'Good Muslim'

Allah (SWT) has explained the qualities of a good Muslim in the Quran, and it is obligatory for all followers to observe them. In practice, because of busy life style and personal commitments it is very difficult to pursue all the guidelines regularly, as stated in the Quran and authentic Hadith. However, it is mandatory for Muslims to follow the main duties without any influence or advocating that they support or follow any of the Hanafi, Shafi, Maliki, Hanbali, or Jaffria schools of thought. Islam dislike any division among believers - anyone who truly accepts 'Shahada' is a Muslim and must follow and practice Quran's guidelines and leave the rest to Allah, who is the final judge of our deeds, and will reward everyone accordingly.

In Surah Baqara C2: V177 qualities of a good Muslim are stated. The following additional attributes are mandatory for all Muslims:

- He (or she) is totally committed, devoted and accepts 'Shahada' that 'There is only one Allah (God)' and there is no one else other than him worth praying to, bowing to or worshipping.

- He (or she) strictly follows the five pillars and six beliefs of Islam, the Quran's and Sunnah/authentic Hadith's guidelines as part of their belief and daily life, and apply them sincerely.

- He (or she) is honest, kind to all human beings and animals, promotes love, peace, unity and tolerance, and does not talk behind people's backs and works hard for their earnings.

- He (or she) is obedient to their parents and looks after them, is kind to orphans, is honest and respects other people's faiths.

- He (or she) reads the Quran with meanings and promotes the messages of Allah (SWT) and last Prophet Muhammad (pbuh) as part of their religious duty, as Islam represents all humanity.

- He (or she) preaches and propagates Islam through Dawah.

9
Benefits of being a 'Devout Muslim'

The benefits of being a good and devout Muslim are enormous: first, you will become a kind, loving and better person in life by understanding the ethics and teachings of Islam. Adherents are advised to avoid imposing personal ideas, religion or superiority on other people, as Islam discourages division and compulsion. It is the belief of all Muslims that there is another life after death, when all human beings' deeds will be accountable and judged according to their behaviours. People who strictly follow Allah's instructions and guidelines as mentioned in the holy book of Quran will be sent to heaven and will enjoy the benefits of their good deeds. Whereas, those who have committed sins and disobeyed Allah's instructions will be severely punished and sent to hell forever.

The ultimate aim for every Muslim should be to earn a place in heaven by being honest and sincerely following Allah's (SWT) instructions as clearly stated in the Quran and authentic hadith. The benefits, beauty of heaven and potential rewards are specifically mentioned in the Surahs Ar-Rehman and Al-Waqia (and in many other surahs), in which Allah (SWT) reminds all human beings of life after death and rewards for those people who are obedient and follow his messages. In the following surah, Allah (SWT) says that:

Surah Al Baqara - C2: V25 *"And give good news*
(O Muhammad) to those who believe and do good deeds that they will
have gardens (Paradise) in which rivers flow..."

"Once, Prophet Muhammad (pbuh) was asked about the paradise (heaven) and he said that guard yourselves from six things, and I am your security for paradise. When you speak, speak the truth; perform when you promise; be trustworthy; be chaste in thought and action; and withhold your hand from striking, and taking or claiming which is unlawful and bad."

10
Things prohibited in Islam

In the Quran, Allah (SWT) has clearly identified specific things forbidden in Islam, and all followers are strongly advised to avoid them and regard them as un-Islamic and immoral. The following is a brief list of prohibited things and the major sins that are unethical for Muslims. Please also see Appendix E for more details.

- Drinking alcohol, eating haram (i.e. pork or meat prepared in an un-Islamic way) and dead animal's meat are prohibited.

- Relationships or love affairs (before and after marriage) are not permitted and regarded as being one of the major sins.

- In Islam, Muslim men and women are not allowed to marry non-Muslims until both male and female sincerely accept and practice Islam. Gay affairs or marriages are also prohibited.

- Forced and underage marriages are forbidden in Islam.

- Muslim women are not allowed to wear transparent or indecent clothes, and must fully cover their body parts as part of Islamic ethics and dress code. Women must also try to avoid wearing excessive makeup, semi naked clothes and imitated men wear that would attract males and initiate evil thoughts.

- Bribing, gambling, betting, fraud, adultery, taking any kind of drugs, and cruelty to people and animals are not allowed.

- Taking interest on capital or savings and obtaining money wrongfully or dishonestly is forbidden in Islam.

- Vulgarity and nudity in any form or shape is not allowed.

- Committing suicide in all circumstances (i.e. because of depression, sense of failure and oppression or for any other reason) is prohibited in Islam. (Ref: Surah An Nisa C4: V29).

- Allah (SWT) does not like those people who are ungrateful, worship other than him, are unkind and cruel.
- Abortion is forbidden in Islam unless the life of the mother is in danger. (Ref: Al Quran C6: V151 and C17: V31).
- Being a gay or men wearing women's clothes is not allowed.
- Avoid listening to vulgar music and watching TV programs, which will encourage and initiate un-Islamic and sinful acts.
- Performing black magic and claiming spiritual or magical cures for mental and physical deficiencies is forbidden.
- Seeking help from self-proclaimed 'fortune-tellers' or 'spiritual healers' about unknown and future matters is forbidden.
- Backbiting and spreading false rumours is forbidden.
- Blasphemy against the Quran and Prophet Muhammad (pbuh) and using offensive words against Islam are regarded as serious crimes and punishable within Islamic laws.
- Suicide attacks, kidnapping, terrorising and killing of innocent people is forbidden in Islam. (Ref. Al Quran C4: V29, C5: V32).
- In addition, Muslims are advised to keep away from those people who are dishonest, untrustworthy, devious and have evil mind, as their un-Islamic, unlawful and immoral activities will cause unnecessary stress and problems for naive people.

In hadith (Sahih Al Bukhari), Prophet Muhammad (pbuh) said that:

"Allah's kindness towards his human beings is more than a mother's towards her child."

"One hour's meditation on the work of the creator is better than seventy years of prayer."

"The best among you are those who read the Quran, understand and follow its teachings, and convey its messages to other people through Dawah (invitation)."

11
Correlation between the Quran and important religious and social issues

It is a known fact that the Quran is a holy book revealed to the last and final Prophet Muhammad (pbuh) over 1400 years ago (between 610 CE and 632 CE) in Mecca and Madina, and contains 114 surahs /chapters (S/C) with 6,236 ayats/verses. The Quran provides complete guidance for humanity and explains religious, social and Islamic issues in details together with benefits and consequences.

In this section, the author identifies some of the real life, social and scientific issues that we face during our life, and occasionally unbelievers ask relevant questions and request further clarification. The following list of important obligations and brief explanations as stated in the Quran will help fellow Muslims to understand and clarify any issue or confusion. You will note that Allah (SWT) has mentioned important issues more than once in various surahs and, therefore, some of the topics discussed are likely to be repeated and mentioned in the Quran to emphasise their significance.

In addition, the author has tried to cross-reference each topic with the relevant surah/ayah and provides a brief explanation in English translation by Mohmmad Pickthall and Yusuf Ali (in italic), so that learned readers are aware of its importance and where in the Quran Allah (SWT) informs about the topic concerned. For more information, it is strongly recommended that readers conduct their own thorough study of the Quran and read other relevant surahs to broaden their own knowledge of a specific subject.

The important religious, social and universe issues listed on the pages (27 to 46) briefly explain and cross-reference each topic with the relevant surah as mentioned in the Quran. You will note that the author has identified some of the life issues and the authentic source for the readers' information. It is, therefore, suggested that the topics covered are used for education and Dawah purposes.

11.1   Religious and Social issues

11.1.1   The existence of God (Allah - SWT)
Al Quran - S/C2: V163, S/C6: V102, V103, S/C112: V1 to V4

It is a primary and total belief of every Muslim that there is only one Almighty God (Allah), who created all human beings, creatures and entire universe. A Muslim cannot be a follower until he or she totally and sincerely accepts the existence of one God, and worship him only. In the following surahs, Allah (SWT) states that:

Surah Al Baqara C2: V163 - *"And your God is One God; there is no God but He, Most Gracious, Most Merciful."*

Surah Al Anaam C6: V102 - *"That is Allah your Lord! There is no God but He, the creator of all things: then worship Him: and He hath power to dispose of all affairs."*

Surah Al Anaam C6: V103 - *"No vision can grasp Him, but His grasp is over all vision: He is above all comprehension, yet is acquainted with all things."*

Surah Al Ikhlas C112: V1 - *"Say: He is Allah, the One and Only;"*

Surah Al Ikhlas C112: V2 - *"Allah, the Eternal, Absolute;"*

Surah Al Ikhlas C112: V3 - *"He begetteth not, nor was He begotten;"*

Surah Al Ikhlas C112: V4 - *"And there is none like unto Him"*

11.1.2 Creation of humankind in the form of Adam (pbuh)
Al Quran - S/C2: V30 to V38, S/C3: V59, S/C7: V11, S/C23: V12-17, S/C49: V13

It is the belief of every Muslim that God (Allah) created human beings in the form of Prophet Adam (pbuh). This faith rejects any other contradictory claims made by Charles Darwin or anybody else. In the following surahs, Allah (SWT) explains the disobedient of Satan/Iblis/Shatan, and how he was ordered to leave heaven:

Surah Al Baqara C2: V30 - *"Behold, thy Lord said to the angels: I will create a vicegerent on earth." They said: "Wilt Thou place therein one who will make mischief therein and shed blood?"...*

Surah Al Baqara C2: V31- *"And He taught Adam the nature of all things; then He placed them before the angels, and said: "Tell me the nature of these if ye are right."*

Surah Al Baqara C2: V33 - *"O Adam! Tell them their natures." When he had told them, Allah said: "Did I not tell you that I know the secrets of heaven and earth, and I know what ye reveal and what ye conceal?"*

Surah Al Baqara C2: V34 - *"And behold, We said to the angels: "Bow down to Adam" and they bowed down. Not so Iblis: he refused and was haughty: He was of those who reject Faith."*

Surah Al Baqara C2: V35 - *"O Adam! Dwell thou and thy wife in the Garden; and eat of the bountiful things therein as (where and when) ye will; but approach not this tree, or ye run into harm and transgression."*

Surah Al Baqara C2: V36 - *"Then did Satan (Iblis) make them slip from the (garden), and get them out of the state (of felicity) in which they had been." We said: "Get ye down, all (ye people), with enmity between yourselves. On earth will be your dwelling-place and your means of livelihood - for a time."*

Surah Al Baqara C2: V38 - *"We said: "Get ye down all from here; and if, as is sure, there comes to you Guidance from me, whosoever follows My guidance, on them shall be no fear, nor shall they grieve."*

Surah Al Imran C3: V59 - *"The similitude of Jesus before Allah is as that of Adam; He created him from dust, then said to him: "Be." And he was"*

Surah Al Araf C7: V11 - *"It is We Who created you and gave you shape; then We bade the angels bow down to Adam, and they bowed down; not so Iblis; He refused to be of those who bow down."*

Surah Al Mominoon C23: V12 - Allah (SWT) says that *"Man We did create from a quintessence (of clay)."*

Surah Al Hujurat C49: V13 - *"O mankind! We created you from a single (pair) of a male and a female, and made you into nations and tribes, that ye may know each other (not that ye may despise (each other). Verily the most honoured of you in the sight of Allah is (he who is) the most righteous of you. And Allah has full knowledge and is well acquainted (with all things)."* (This surah disapproves the theory of evolution.)

11.1.3   Satan's/Shatan /Iblis/Devil's disobedience
Al Quran - S/C2: V34, S/C7: V12 to V18, S/C17: V61 to V65, S/C18: V50

In the following surahs, Allah (SWT) clearly mentions Satan's refusal to obey his commandment and disobedience:

Surah Al Araf C7: V13 - *(Allah) said: "Get thee down from this: it is not for thee to be arrogant here: get out, for thou art of the meanest ..."*

Surah Bani Israil C17: V61 - *"Behold! We said to the angels: "Bow down unto Adam": They bowed down except Iblis: He said, "Shall I bow down to one whom Thou didst create from clay?"*

Surah Al Kahf C18: V50 - *"Behold! We said to the angels, "Bow down to Adam": They bowed down except Iblis. He was one of the Jinns, and he broke the Command of his Lord..."*

11.1.4 Shahada/Tauheed - accepting one true deity (God)
Al Quran - S/C2: V163, S/C3: V18, S/C6: V102, V103, S/C112: V1 to V4

Shahada is the first pillar of Islam and mandatory for every Muslim to accept and practice in real life. This is the essence of Islam and without this belief; a person cannot be accepted as a Muslim. In the following surahs, Allah (SWT) explains about Shahada/Tauheed:

Surah Al Baqara C2: V163 - *"And your Allah is One Allah. There is no God but He, Most Gracious, Most Merciful."*

Surah Al Imran C3: V18 - *"There is no god but He: That is the witness of Allah, His angels, and those endued with knowledge, standing firm on justice. There is no god but He, the Exalted in Power"*

Surah Al Anaam C6: V102 - *"That is Allah, your Lord! There is no God but He, the creator of all things: then worship Him: and He hath power to dispose of all affairs."*

Surah Al Hadid C57: V4 - *..."Allah is with you wherever you are..."*

Surah Al Ikhlas C112: V1 - *"Say: He is Allah, the One and Only;"*

Surah Al Ikhlas C112: V2 - *"Allah, the Eternal, Absolute;"*

Surah Al Ikhlas C112: V3 - *"He begetteth not, nor is He begotten;"*

Surah Al Ikhlas C112: V4 - *"And there is none like unto Him."*

11.1.5   Salah/Salat - praying five times a day
Al Quran - S/C17: V78, S/C30: V17, V18, S/C73: V20

Salah is the second pillar of Islam, and it is obligatory for Muslims to pray 5 times a day (at different times) between early morning and late evening. In the following surahs, Allah informs about Salah:

Surah Al Isra C17: V78 - *"Establish regular prayers - at the sunset till the darkness of the night, and the Morning Prayer and reading: for the prayer and reading in the morning carry their testimony."*

Surah Ar Room C30: V17 - *"So (give) glory to Allah, when ye reach eventide and when ye rise in the morning"*

Surah Ar Room C30: V18 - *"Yea, to Him be praise, in the heavens and on earth; and in the late afternoon and when the sun's decline."*

Surah Al Muzzammil C73: V20 - *"... and observe the SALAT and ZAKAT, and lend God a loan of righteousness. Whatever you advance for your souls, you will find at God better and multiplied manifold..."*

11.1.6   Zakat – helping the poor and needy
Al Quran - S/C2:245, S/C2:277, S/C9:103, S/C51:19, S/C24:56, S/C73:20, S/C98:5

Zakat is the third pillar of Islam and all Muslims are obliged to give 2.5% of their wealth and savings to poor and needy people every year. This obligatory duty is a great way to distribute wealth within the family members and community, and helping deprived and less fortunate people. In the following surahs, Allah (SWT) informs followers of Islam about Zakat and its benefits here after:

Surah Al Baqara C2: V245 - *"Who is he that will loan to Allah a beautiful loan, which Allah will double unto his credit and multiply many times? It is Allah that giveth (you) Want or plenty..."*

Surah Al Baqara C2: V277 - *"Those who believe, and do good work, and establish regular prayers and regular charity, will have their reward with their Lord: on them shall be no fear, nor shall they grieve."*

Surah Al Muzzammil C73: V20 - *"... and observe the SALAT and ZAKAT, and lend God a loan of righteousness. Whatever you advance for your souls, you will find at God better and multiplied manifold..."*

11.1.7   Sawm - fasting during the month of Ramadan
Al Quran - S/C2: V183, V184 and V185

Sawm is the fourth pillar of Islam and prescribed for Muslims during the month of Ramadan, and followers are advised to fast and pray for one month. Vast majority of Muslims fast and do not eat or drink anything from dawn until sunset. This sacrifice is carried out for Allah (SWT), expressing gratitude to him for his kindness and mercy. In the following surahs, Allah (SWT) instructs Muslims about fasting during the holy month of Ramadan:

Surah Al Baqara C2: V183 - *"O ye who believe! Fasting is prescribed to you as it was prescribed to those before you, that ye may (learn) self-restraint."*

Surah Al Baqara C2: V184 - *"(Fasting) for a fixed number of days; but if any of you is ill, or on a journey, the prescribed number (Should be made up) from days later. For those who can do it (With hardship), is a ransom, the feeding of one that is indigent. However, he that will give more, of his own free will - it is better for him. And it is better for you that ye fast, if ye only knew."*

Surah Al Baqara C2: V185 - *"Ramadan is the (month) in which was sent down the Qur'an, as a guide to mankind, also clear (Signs) for guidance and judgment (Between right and wrong). So every one of you who is present (at his home) during that month should spend it in fasting, but if any one is ill, or on a journey, the prescribed period (Should be made up) by days later. Allah intends every facility for you..."*

11.1.8   Performing Hajj (pilgrimage to Mecca)
Al Quran - S/C 2: V196, S/C3: V96-97, S/C22: V26 to V28

Hajj is the fifth pillar of Islam and is obligatory for every Muslim, who is financially and physically capable to carry out pilgrimage to Mecca to perform Hajj ritual. It is the wish of every Muslim to fulfil their religious duty once in a lifetime. In the following surahs, Allah (SWT) informs Muslims to perform Hajj:

Surah Al Baqara C2: V196 - *"Perform pilgrimage and visit (to Khana Kaaba - Mecca) for Allah..."*

Surah Al Imran C3: V96 - *"The first House (of worship) appointed for mankind was that at Bakka (Mecca): Full of blessing and of guidance for all peoples."*

Surah Al Imran C3: V97 - *"In it are Signs Manifest; (for example), the Station of Abraham; whoever enters it attains security; Pilgrimage thereto is a duty men owe to Allah - those who can afford the journey; but if any deny faith, Allah stands not in need of any of His creatures."*

11.1.9   How to perform Vuzu (cleaning) prior to praying
Al Quran - S/C5: V6

It is obligatory for Muslims to clean themselves prior to performing a salah or reading the Quran. The following surah briefly explains how to clean and wash before praying:

Surah Al Maidah C5: V6 - *"O ye who believe! When ye rise up for prayer, wash your faces, and your hands up to the elbows, and lightly rub your heads and (wash) your feet up to the ankles. If you are unclean, purify yourselves. And if you are sick or on a journey, or one of you cometh from the closet, or ye have had (sexual) contact with women, and ye find not water, then go to clean, high ground and rub your faces and your hands with some of it. Allah would not place a burden on you, but He would purify you and would perfect His grace upon you... "*

11.1.10   Belief in Allah's books, prophets and angels
Al Quran - S/C3: V67, V84; S/C21: V26, V27; S/C66: V6

All Muslims belief in prophets, angels and books revealed by God (Allah) and anybody disregard these faiths cannot become or claim to be a Muslim. In the following surahs, Allah (SWT) explains that:

Surah Al Imran C3: V67 - *"Abraham was not a Jew nor yet a Christian; but he was true in Faith, and bowed his will to Allah's (Which is Islam), and he was not of the idolaters."*

Surah Al Imran C3: V84 -   *Say: "We believe in Allah, and in what has been revealed to us and what was revealed to Abraham, Isma'il, Isaac, Jacob, and the Tribes, and in (the Books) given to Moses, Jesus, and the prophets, from their Lord: We make no distinction between one and another among them, and to Allah do we bow our will (in Islam)."*

Surah Al Anbiya C21: V26 - 27 - *"They (Angels) are but honored servants; they speak not until He has spoken; and they act by His (Allah's) command."*

Surah Al Tahrim C66: V6 - *"The Angels never disobey Allah, who disobey not the command they receive from Allah, but do that which they are told."*

11.1.11 Marriage in Islam
Al Quran - S/C2: V221, S/C4: V3, V23, S/C24: V26 - 27, V32

Marriage is regarded as an important part of life in Islam and in the Quran, Allah (SWT) advise whom a Muslim can and cannot marry. It is important that both men and women have the full blessing and consent of their parents before marrying or deciding whom they wish to marry. Both boys and girls must be consulted before parents decide or choose their future partner, as forced and marriages without consent are not permitted in Islam.

Surah Al Baqara C2: V221 - *"Do not marry unbelieving women (idolaters), until they believe: A slave women who believe is better than an unbelieving woman even though she allures you. Nor marry (your girls) to unbelievers until they believe: A man slave who believes is better than an unbeliever, even though he allures you..."*

Surah An Nisa C4: V3 - *"If ye fear that ye shall not be able to deal justly with the orphans, Marry women of your choice, Two or three or four; but if ye fear that ye shall not be able to deal justly (with them), then only one, or (a captive) that your right hands possess, that will be more suitable, to prevent you from doing injustice."*

Surah An Nisa C4: V23 - *"Prohibited to you (For marriage) are: Your mothers, daughters, sisters; father's sisters, Mother's sisters; brother's daughters, sister's daughters; foster-mothers, foster-sisters; your wives' mothers; your step-daughters under your guardianship, wives of your sons proceeding from your loins; and two sisters in wedlock at one and the same time, except for what is past..."*

Surah An-Noor C24: V26 - *"Vile women are for vile men, and vile men for vile women. Good women are for good men and good men are for good women..."* (This surah advises Muslims to choose partners wisely.)

11.1.12   Divorce in Islam
Al Quran - S/C2: V229 to V237, S/C65: V1 to V7

In Islam, divorce is not encouraged (except in exceptional cases), and regarded as a social stigma and a complex issue. In fact, Islam is the only religion, which advises its followers to marry once in a lifetime and avoid divorce. It is, therefore, suggested that the other relevant surahs are also read and understood, and (if required) an Ulma (a Muslim scholar) is consulted before making any decision. The following surahs briefly explain the importance of divorce:

Surah Al Baqara C2: V229 - *"A divorce is only permissible twice: after that, the parties should either hold together on equitable terms, or separate with kindness. It is not lawful for you, (Men), to take back any of your gifts (from your wives), except when both parties fear that they would be unable to keep the limits ordained by Allah. If ye (judges) do indeed fear that they would be unable to keep the limits ordained by Allah, there is no blame on either of them if she gives something for her freedom. These are the limits ordained by Allah. So do not transgress them if any do transgress the limits ordained by Allah..."*

Surah Al Baqara C2: V230 - *"So if a husband divorces his wife (irrevocably), He cannot, after that, re-marry her until after she has married another husband and He has divorced her. In that case there is no blame on either of them if they re-unite; provided they feel that they can keep the limits ordained by Allah. Such are the limits ordained by Allah, which He makes plain to those who understand."*

11.1.13   Hajab/Veil /Purda
Al Quran - S/C24: V30, V31, S/C33: V59

Hajab is a religious obligation and Muslim women are prohibited to wear transparent or indecent clothes, and advised to fully cover their body as part of Islamic dress code and ethics. Women must also try to avoid wearing excessive makeup and cloths that would imitate men wear. In the following surahs, women are instructed not to encourage and be friendly with non-blood related males:

Surah An Noor C24: V30 - *"Tell the believing men to lower their gaze and be modest. This is purer for them..."*

Surah An Noor C24: V31 - *"And say to the believing women that they should lower their gaze and guard their modesty; that they should not display their beauty and ornaments except what (must ordinarily) appear thereof; that they should draw their veils over their bosoms and not display their beauty except to their husbands, their fathers, their husband's fathers, their sons, their husbands' sons, their brothers or their brothers' sons, or their sisters' sons, or their women or the slaves whom their right hands possess, or male servants ..."*

Surah Al Ahzab C33: V59 - *"O Prophet! Tell thy wives and daughters, and the believing women, that they should cast their outer garments over their persons (when abroad): that is most convenient, that they should be known (as such) and not molested..."*

11.1.14   Women's role in Islam
Al Quran - S/C2: V187, S/C4: V34; S/C9: V71, S/C16: V97, S/C30: V21, C33: V35

In the following surahs, Allah (SWT) briefly explains the role of women in Islam as being a sister, a wife and a mother, and that their contribution is well respected and recognized. The Quran clearly states that men and women who practice Islam and follow the Quran's and Hadith's guidelines will receive equal rewards for their efforts; this means that women's role is equal to men in Islam and there is no degrading or disrespect to women:

Surah Al Baqara C2: V187 - *"They (women) are garments for you while you are garments for them."*

Surah An Nisa C4: V34 - *"Men are the protectors and maintainers of women, because Allah has given the one more (strength) than the other, and because they support them from their means. Therefore the righteous women are devoutly obedient, and guard in (the husband's) absence what Allah would have them guard..."*

Surah Al Tauba C9: V71 - *"The Believers, men and women, are protectors one of another: they enjoin what is just and forbid what is evil: they observe regular prayers, practice regular charity, and obey Allah and His Messenger. On them will Allah pour His mercy: for Allah is exalted in power, Wise"* (This surah re-emphasise the essence of Islam.)

Surah Al Nahl C16: V97 - *"Whosoever performs good deeds, whether male or female, and is a believer, We shall surely make him live a good life, and We will certainly reward them for the best of what they did"*

Surah AnNoor C24: V26 - *"Vile women are for vile men, and vile men for vile women. Good men are for good women and good women are for good men..."* (This surah advises Muslims to choose their partners wisely).

Surah Ar Room C30: V21 - *"Among His signs is (the fact) that He has created spouses for you from among yourselves so that you may console yourselves with them. He has planted love and mercy between you; in that are signs for people who reflect."*

Surah Al Ahzab C33: V35 - *"For Muslim men and women, for believing men and women, for devout men and women, for true men and women, for men and women who are patient and constant, for men and women who humble themselves, for men and women who give in charity, for men and women who fast, for men and women who guard their chastity, and for men and women who engage much in Allah's praise, for them has Allah prepared forgiveness and great reward."*

11.1.15 Respect and caring for parents
Al Quran - S/C17: V23, V24, S/C46: V15

In Islam, parents respect and caring is an obligatory duty for Muslims, and children are advised to be kind and look after them in their lifetime and old age. Both father and mother holds a special place in Islam, but a mother's role and sacrifice is more recognised and rewarded. In a Hadith (Sahih Al Bukhari), it is narrated that a man came to Prophet Muhammed (pbuh) and asked:

"Messenger of Allah, who is the most deserving of good care from me?" The Prophet Muhammed (pbuh) replied: 'Your mother' (the man asked the same question three times and prophet repeated three times - Your mother) then your father, then your nearest relatives in order."

In another Hadith (Sahih Al-Bukhari) the Prophet Muhammad (pbuh) said: "Paradise lies at the feet of mothers." In other words, paradise awaits those who cherish and respect their mothers.

In the following surahs, Allah (SWT) states that respecting parents and looking after them is part of children's duty:

Surah Al Isra C17: V23 - *"Thy Lord hath decreed that ye worship none but Him, and that ye be kind to parents. Whether one or both of them attain old age in thy life, say not to them a word of contempt, nor repel them, but address them in terms of honour."*

Surah Al Isra C17: V24 - *"And, out of kindness, lower to them the wing of humility, and say: My Lord! Bestow on them thy Mercy even as they cherished me in childhood."*

Surah Al Ahqaf C46: V15 - *"We have enjoined on man kindness to his parents: In pain did his mother bear him, and in pain did she give him birth. The carrying of the (child) to his weaning is (a period of) thirty months. At length, when he reaches the age of full strength and attains forty years, he says, O my Lord! Grant me that I may be grateful for Thy favor which Thou has bestowed upon me, and upon both my parents, and that I may work righteousness such as Thou mayest approve; and be gracious to me in my issue. Truly have I turned to Thee and truly do I bow (to Thee) in Islam."*

11.1.16   Halal and Haram in Islam
Al Quran - S/C2: V172, V173

Islam strongly instructs Muslims to avoid eating certain meats and foods, which are prepared un-Islamic way and prohibited for its followers. In the western world, Muslims are advised to take extra care when ordering meals from fast food chains or restaurants. In the following surahs, Allah (SWT) informs Muslims about halal and haram (un-Islamic) things, which are specifically forbidden:

Surah Al Baqara C2: V172 - *"O ye who believe! Eat of the good things that We have provided for you, and be grateful to Allah..."*

Surah Al Baqara C2: V173 - *"He hath only forbidden you dead meat, and blood, and the flesh of swine, and that on which any other name hath been invoked besides that of Allah. However, if one is forced by necessity, without willful disobedience, nor transgressing due limits - then is he guiltless. For Allah is Often-forgiving Most Merciful."*

11.1.17   Usury/Riba/Interest
Al Quran - S/C2: V276 to V280, S/C3: V130, S/C4: V161, S/C30: V39

In Islam, Usury or Riba means earning interest on personal savings, wealth and property assets, etc. In the following surahs, Allah (SWT) informs Muslims about Usury/Riba and its repercussions:

Surah Al Baqara C2: V276 to V280 - *"GOD condemns usury, and blesses charities. O you who believe, you shall observe GOD and refrain from all kinds of usury, if you are believers. If you do not, then expect a war from GOD and His messenger. However, if you repent, you may keep your capitals, without inflicting injustice, or incurring injustice. If the debtor is unable to pay, wait for a better time. If you give up the loan as a charity, it would be better for you, if you only knew."*

Surah Al Imran C3: V130 - *"... you shall not take usury/interest, compounded over and over. Observe GOD that you may succeed."*

Surah An Nisa C4: V161 - *"And for practicing usury, which was forbidden, and for consuming the people's money illicitly. We have prepared for the disbelievers among them painful retribution."*

Surah Ar Room C30: V39 - *"The usury that is practiced to increase some people's wealth, does not gain anything at GOD. But if you give to charity, seeking God's pleasure, these are the ones who receive their reward manifold."*

11.1.18   Punishments in Islam
Al Quran - S/C5: V38, S/C24: V2 to V4

In the following surahs, Allah (SWT) informs Muslims about the major crimes and expected punishments within the Islamic laws:

Surah Al Maidah C5: V38 - *"As to the thief, Male or female cut off his or her hands: a punishment by way of example, from Allah, for their crime: and Allah is exalted in power."*

Surah An Noor C24: V2 - *"The woman and the man guilty of adultery or fornication, - flog each of them with a hundred stripes: Let not compassion move you in their case, in a matter prescribed by Allah, if ye believe in Allah and the Last Day: and let a party of the Believers witness their punishment."* (This surah will help to deter major crimes.)

Surah An Noor C24: V3 - *"Let no man guilty of adultery or fornication marries and but a woman similarly guilty, or an Unbeliever: nor let any but such a man or an Unbeliever marries such a woman: to the Believers such a thing is forbidden."*

Surah An Noor C24: V4 - *"And those who launch a charge against chaste women, and produce not four witnesses (to support their allegations), - flog them with eighty stripes; and reject their evidence ever after: for such men are wicked transgressors."*

11.1.19 Jihad and Shaheed/Martyrs
Al Quran - S/C2: V190, S/C3: V157

In Islam, Jihad means 'struggle and strive' and it is obligatory for Muslims to make financial and physical sacrifice for protecting Islam, fighting for justice, freedom, human rights and advocating Islamic ethics and Quran's teachings. The following surahs states:

Surah Al Baqara C2: V190 - *"Fight in the cause of Allah those who fight you, but do not disobey limits; for Allah loveth not transgressors."*

Surah Al Imran C3: V157 - *"And if ye are slain, or die, in the way of Allah, forgiveness from Allah are far better than all they could amass."*

11.1.20 Suicide and killing of innocent human beings
Al Quran – S/C4: V29, S/C5: V32

In Islam, suicide attacks, terrorising and killing of innocent people is prohibited and condemned. These acts are classified as major sins, un-Islamic and unforgivable, and must therefore be avoided. People who pursue such appalling acts are brainwashed and motivated to execute their personal grievances. In addition, in the West, suicide killing is unjustly linked with Islam, holy war and jihad. This is a wrong perception. In the following surahs, Allah (SWT) tells that:

Surah An Nisa C4: V29 - *"… and do not kill yourselves (nor kill one another.) Surely Allah is Most merciful to you."*

Surah Al Maida C5: V32 - *"If anyone killed a person, unless it was for murder or spreading mischief on earth, it would be as if he killed all of mankind. And if anyone saved a life, it would be as if he had saved the lives of all mankind."* (The above surahs prohibits suicide killing.)

11.1.21   Abortion in Islam
Al Quran - S/C6: V151, S/C 17: V31

Abortion is a controversial subject and is strictly not allowed in Islam, and must therefore be avoided. However, in exceptional cases when a mother's life is in danger then (in such circumstances) a fetus or unborn child can be aborted to save the life of the mother. In the following surahs, Allah (SWT) instructs about abortion:

Surah Al Anaam C6: V151 - *"...And that ye slay (kill) not the life which Allah hath made sacred, save in the course of justice. This He hath command you, in order that ye may discern."*

Surah Al Isra C17: V31 - *"Slay (kill) not your children, fearing a fall to poverty, We shall provide for them and for you."*

11.1.22   Judaism and Christianity
Al Quran - S/C3: V84, S/C17: V2

Both Judaism and Christianity are well respected in Islam, and known as Abrahamic religions. In Islam, both these faiths are treated with great respect and Prophet Abraham, Moses and Jesus are regarded as prophets of God. In the following surahs, Allah (SWT) informs about various religions and books, which were revealed to other prophets for their respective tribes and nations.

Surah Al Imran C3: V84 - Say *"We believe in Allah, and in what has been revealed to us and what was revealed to Abraham, Isma'il, Isaac, Jacob, and the Tribes, and in (the Books) given to Moses, Jesus, and the prophets, from their Lord: We make no distinction between one and another among them, and to Allah do we bow our will (in Islam)."*

Surah Al Isra C17: V2 - *"We gave Moses the Book, and made it a Guide to the Children of Israel..."*

11.1.23   Life after death - Heaven and Hell
Al Quran - S/C2:24, 25, S/C3:91,185, S/C4:57, S/C6:27, S/C57:21, S/C7, C55, C56

It is one of the Muslims faiths that there is a life after death, when all human beings will be resurrected and judged according to their good and bad deeds, and rewarded and punished accordingly.

In the following surahs, Allah (SWT) reminds about life after death. In Surahs Ar-Rehman and Al-Waqia C55 and C56, Allah (SWT) fully explains and reminds human beings about Heaven and Hell. It is strongly recommended that one should study the full contents and try to understand the messages that Allah (SWT) conveys to us together with the rewards and punishments:

Surah Al Baqara C2: V24 - *"But if ye cannot- and of a surety ye cannot- then fear the Fire whose fuel is men and stones- which is prepared for those who reject Faith."*

Surah Al Baqara C2: V25 - *"But give glad tidings to those who believe and work righteousness, that their portion is Gardens, beneath which rivers flow. Every time they are fed with fruits there from, they say: "Why, this is what we were fed with before," for they are given things in similitude; and they have therein companions pure)."*

Surah Al Imran C3: V91 - *"As to those who reject Faith, and die rejecting,- never would be accepted from any such as much gold as the earth contains, though they should offer it for ransom. For such is (in store) a penalty grievous, and they will find no helpers."*

Surah Al Imran C3: V185 - *"Every soul shall have a taste of death: And only on the Day of Judgment shall you be paid your full recompense. Only he who is saved far from the Fire and admitted to the Garden will have attained the object (of Life): For the life of this world is but goods and chattels of deception."*

Surah Al Nisa C4: V57 - *"But those who believe and do deeds of righteousness, We shall soon admit to Gardens, with rivers flowing beneath,- their eternal home: Therein shall they have companions pure and holy: We shall admit them to shades, cool and ever deepening."*

11.1.24   End of life on earth (i.e. Qyamat)
Al Quran – S/C 29:V57, S/C31:34, S/C36: V51, V53, S/C56 V4 to V6

In the Quran, Allah (SWT) reminds all human beings about the end of life on earth, and indicates some of the major signs before it will occur. In the following surahs, Allah (SWT) informs about the Qyamat (final judgment day/end of life) and how it will happen. Only Allah (SWT) knows the time, and when it will happen:

Surah Al Ankabut C29: V57 - *"Every soul will taste of death. Then unto Us ye will be returned"*

Surah Luqman C31: V34 - *"Surely, knowledge of the Hour (judgment day) is with Allah alone..."*

Surah Yaseen C36:V51 - *"The trumpet shall be sounded, when behold! from the sepulchers (men) will rush forth to their Lord!"*

Surah Yaseen C36: V53 - *"It will be no more than a single blast, when lo! They will all be brought up before Us"*

Surah Al Waqia C56: V4 and V5 *"When the earth shall be shaken to its depths,"* – V5 *"And the mountains shall be crumbled to atoms/dust,"*

Surah Al Waqia C56: V6 - *"Becoming dust scattered abroad"*

11.1.25   The day of judgment
Al Quran - S/C3: V185, S/C36: V50 to V56

Once again, Allah (SWT) has clearly indicated the final judgment day in the Quran; there are many other surahs, which highlight the importance of this day. It is one of the Muslim beliefs that the final judgment time will certainly come one day, whenever Allah (SWT) decides, it will happen instantly without any warning. In the following surahs, Allah (SWT) reminds us about the final judgment day, rewards and punishments expected according to our deeds:

Surah Al Imran C3: V185 - *"Every soul shall have a taste of death: And only on the Day of Judgment shall you be paid your full recompense. Only he who is saved far from the Fire and admitted to the Garden will have attained the object (of Life): For the life of this world is but goods and chattels of deception."*

Surah Yaseen C36: V50 - *"No (chance) will they then have, by will, to dispose (of their affairs), nor to return to their own people!"*

Surah Yaseen C36: V51 - *"The trumpet shall be sounded, when behold! from the sepulchers (men) will rush forth to their Lord!"*

Surah Yaseen C36: V52 - *"They will say: "Ah! Woe unto us! Who hath raised us up from our beds of repose?"... (A voice will say:) "This is what (Allah) Most Gracious had promised. And true was the word of the apostles!"*

Surah Yaseen C36: V53, 54, 55 and V56 - *"It will be no more than a single Blast, when lo! they will all be brought up before Us!"*- *"Then, on that Day, not a soul will be wronged in the least, and ye shall but be repaid the needs of your past Deeds."* V55 - *"Verily the Companions of the Garden shall that Day have joy in all that they do;"* V56 - *"They and their associates will be in cool shade, reclining on Thrones (of dignity);"*

11.1.26 Various phrases used by Muslims in their daily life
(ie. Assalama o Alaikum, Alhumdolilha, Insha-Allah, Mashallah, etc.)

Muslims generally use various Arabic phrases in their daily life to greet each other or during their usual conversation. This is a normal practice and praises Allah (SWT) for his supremacy and blessing. In the following surahs, some of the phrases are briefly explained:

'Assalama o Alaikum' - 'Islamic greeting meaning peace be upon you'- Ref: Surah Al Anam C6: V54 - *"And those who believe in Our revelations come unto thee, say: Assalama o Alaikum - Peace be unto you!"*

'Alhumdolilha' - meaning 'All praise belongs to Allah' - Ref: Surah Abraham C14: V39 - *"Praise be to Allah Who hath given me..."*

'Insha-Allah' - meaning 'Allah willing' - Ref: Surah Al Khaf C18: V23 - *"And say not of everything; Lo! I shall do that tomorrow"*

'Mashallah' - meaning 'by the grace of Allah' - Ref: Surah Al-Ala - C87: V7 - *"Unless Allah wishes; He knows both what is open and what is hidden".* (This phrase re-emphasise the beauty of Allah (God).

'Darood' (blessing) - Ref: Surah Al Ahzab C33: V56 - *"Allah and His angels send blessings on the Prophet: O ye that believe! Send ye blessings on him, and salute (salam) him with all respect."*

11.2   Scientific and Universe issues

11.2.1   Six days of creation - origin of the universe
Al Quran – S/C10: V3, S/C21: V30 to V33, S/C32: V4, S/C57: V4

The following surahs briefly inform human beings about the universe, and how it was created within six days:

Surah Yunus C10: V3 - *"Lo! your Lord is Allah Who created the heavens and earth in six days..."*

Surah Al Anbiya C21: V30 - *"Do not the Unbelievers see that the heavens and the earth were joined together (as one unit), before we clove them asunder? We made from water every living thing…"*

Surah Al Anbiya C21: V31 - *"And We have set on the earth mountains standing firm, lest it should shake with them, and We have made therein broad highways (between mountains) for them to pass through: that they may receive Guidance."*

Surah Al Anbiya C21: V32 - *"And We have made the heavens as a canopy well guarded: yet do they turn away from the signs which these things (point to)!"*

Surah Al Anbiya C21: V33 - *"It is He Who created the Night and the Day, and the sun and the moon: all (the celestial bodies) swim along, each in its rounded course."*

Surah As Sajdah C32: V4 - *"It is Allah Who has created the heavens and the earth, and all between them, in six Days, and is firmly established on the Throne (of Authority): ye have none, besides Him, to protect or intercede (for you): will ye not then receive admonition?"*

Surah Al Hadid C57: V4 - *"He it is Who created the heavens and the earth in Six Days, and is moreover firmly established on the Throne (of Authority). He knows what enters within the earth and what comes forth out of it, what comes down from heaven and what mounts up to it. And He is with you wherever ye may be. And Allah sees well all that ye do."*

11.2.2 The nature of soul - human embryonic development
Al Quran - S/C22: V5, S/C23: V12 to V14

In the following surahs, Allah (SWT) explains about the human embryonic development and the birth of a child:

Surah Al Hajj C22: V5 - *"O mankind! if ye have a doubt about the Resurrection, then lo! We have created you from dust, then from a drop of seed, then out of a leech-like clot, then from a clot, partly formed and partly unformed, in order that We may manifest (our power) to you; and We cause whom We will to rest in the wombs for an appointed term, then do We bring you out as infants, then (foster you) that ye may reach your age of full strength; and some of you are called to die, and some are sent back to the feeblest old age, so that they know nothing after having known (much), and (further), thou seest the earth barren and lifeless, but when We pour down rain on it, it is stirred (to life)…"*

Surah Al Mominoon C23: V12 - *"Man We did create from a quintessence (of clay)"*

Surah Al Mominoon C23: V13 - *"Then We placed him as (a drop of) sperm in a place of rest, firmly fixed,"*

Surah Al Mominoon C23: V14 - *"Then We made the sperm into a clot of congealed blood; then of that clot We made a lump; then we made out of that lump bones and clothed the bones with flesh; then we developed out of it another creature. So blessed be Allah, the best to create!"*

11.2.3 Laws of nature - clouds, rain, seas, mountains, water
Al Quran - S/C23: V18, V19, S/C24: V43

The following surahs briefly explain the laws of nature:

Surah Al Mominoon C23: V18 - *"And We sends down water from the sky according to (due) measure, and We cause it to soak in the soil; and We certainly are able to drain it off (with ease)."*

Surah Al Mominoon C23: V19 - *"With it We grow for you gardens of date-palms and vines: in them have ye abundant fruits: and of them ye eat (and have enjoyment)."*

Surah An Noor C24: V43 - *"Seest thou not that Allah makes the clouds move gently, then joins them together, then makes them into a heap? - then wilt thou see rain issue forth from their midst. And He sends down from the sky mountain masses (of clouds) wherein is hail: He strikes therewith whom He pleases and He turns it away from whom He pleases, the vivid flash of His lightning well-nigh blinds the sight."*

11.2.4 Sun, moon, day and night
Al Quran - S/C24: V44, S/C39: V5

In the following surahs, Allah (SWT) instructs human beings about the routine functions of the sun, moon, day and night:

Surah An Noor C24: V44 - *"It is Allah Who alternates the Night and the Day: verily in these things is an instructive example for those who have vision!"*

Surah Az Zumar C39: V5 - *"He created the heavens and the earth in true (proportions): He makes the Night overlap the Day, and the Day overlap the Night: He has subjected the sun and the moon (to His law): Each one follows a course for a time appointed. Is not He the Exalted in Power - He who forgives again and again?"*

11.2.5 Creation of life on earth from water
Al Quran - S/C21: V30, S/C24: V45, S/C25: V54,

In the following surahs, Allah (SWT) informs about the creation of life on the earth from water. These surahs also disapprove the controversial and scientifically unproven theory of evolution:

Surah Al Anbiya C21: V30 - *"Do not the unbelievers see that the heavens and the earth were joined together (as one unit of creation), before we clove them asunder? We made from water every living thing. Will they not then believe?"*

Surah An Noor C24: V45 - *"And Allah has created every animal from water: of them there are some that creep on their bellies; some that walk on two legs; and some that walk on four. Allah creates what He wills for verily Allah has power over all things."*

Surah Al Furqan C25: V54 - *"It is He who has created man from water: then has He established relationships of lineage and marriage: for thy Lord has power (over all things)."*

In Surah Yusuf C12: V2 Allah (SWT) states that:
"We have sent it down as an Arabic Qur'an, in order that you may learn wisdom."

Did you know?
In the Quran only 25 prophets' names have been stated, and it is obligatory for Muslims to respect them all. Prophet Musa's (Moses) name is top of the list and mentioned 136 times; Prophet Abraham's name is listed 69 times, Prophet Jesus name is listed 29 times, and Prophet Muhammad's name is stated only 4 times.

12
Miracles performed by the prominent prophets as stated in the Quran

In the Quran Allah (SWT) clearly mentions the miracles and special qualities and responsibilities he provided to his prophets. It is a fact that in order to persuade unbelievers of the existence of the one and only Almighty Allah (God) and his messages, the majority of the prophets performed various miracles with the help and blessing of Allah (SWT). Even after persistent challenges and requests for proofs and miracles, unbelievers did not accept Islam and accused prophets of being 'magicians', but all messengers (because of the special blessing from Allah (SWT) and their total belief) continued preaching Allah's (SWT) teachings and messages without any fear and with total commitment, love and passion. As a result, Islam continued to spread throughout the Arab land, and today is the fastest growing religion in the world.

In the following surah, Allah (SWT) briefly mentions the miracles performed by the prophets:

Surah AnKabut C29: V50 - *"Say (O Muhammad): The signs (Miracles) are indeed with Allah: and most certainly I am only a clear Warner!"*

The following is a summary of the famous miracles performed by the prominent prophets as mentioned in the Quran.

12.1 Miracles associated with Prophet Ibrahim (pbuh)

In the following Surah Al-Anbia C21: V69, Allah (SWT) instructs about the **'Fire'** miracle, and He said:

"O fire! Be coolness and peace for Ibrahim."

In this miracle, after Prophet Ibrahim (Abraham) (pbuh) broke the unbelievers' statues/idols they punished him and decided to throw him into a pit of fire that they specially prepared for him. Prophet Ibrahim (pbuh) prayed to Allah (SWT) for his help, and he with full faith, confidence and without any fear walked on to it, and the fire pit turned into flowers. Because of this miracle, unbelievers were astonished, but once again, they did not accept Islam and accused Prophet Ibrahim (pbuh) of being a 'magician'.

In another famous miracle Prophet Ibrahim (pbuh) had a dream in which he was asked to sacrify his most precious and loved thing for the sake of Allah (SWT). Prophet Ibrahim (pbuh) continuously had the same dream for three days and was worried and indecisive. He discussed the dream with his wife (Bibi Hajira) and son Ismail, and with their full consent took his son to the desert (a few miles out of Mecca to the desert Minna), and put a piece of cloth on his body (covering all parts) and tried to sacrify his son's life by cutting his throat. As he tried, Allah (SWT) performed a miracle, and Ismail was placed with a goat and he stood next to his father unharmed. This miracle showed total obedience and adherence to Allah's (SWT) instructions, and both Prophet Ibrahim (pbuh) and his son followed the message without any panic or fear. In return, Allah (SWT) rewarded both Prophet Ibrahim and his son with the great gift of remembrance through the annual festival of Eid ul Azha, when after the Hajj rituals Muslims (Hajji) sacrify a halal animal like a goat, sheep, camel or a cow/buffalo, as part of their religious duty. (It is worth restating that Hajj is the fifth pillar of Islam and obligatory for Muslims.)

One day Prophet Ibrahim (pbuh) begged Allah to show him how he would bring the dead back to life. Allah (SWT) instructed Prophet Ibrahim (pbuh) to take four birds, cut them up and mix their body parts, divide them into four portions and place them on top of four different hills, then call back the birds in Allah's name. Prophet Ibrahim (pbuh) followed the instructions. Immediately, all mixed parts of the birds started to separate and joined their original bodies in different places and the birds flew back to him.

Allah (SWT) revealed this miracle in Surah Al Baqara C2: V260:

Remember when Ibrhaim said:
"My Lord, show me how You give life to the dead." Allah said: "Do
you not believe?" Ibrahim said: "Yes I believe, but to be stronger in
Faith." He said: "Take four birds, the cause them to incline towards
you (then slaughter them, cut them into pieces) and then put a
portion of them on every hill and call them they will come to you in
haste. And know that Allah is All Mighty and All Wise."

12.2   Miracles performed by Prophet Musa (pbuh)

In Surah Al Baqara C2: V60, Allah (SWT) informs about the water miracle, when Prophet Musa (Moses) (pbuh) prayed for water on behalf of his people and Allah (SWT) said:

"Strike the rock with thy staff (stick). Then gushed forth there from
twelve springs, each group knew its own place for water. So eat and
drink of the sustenance provided by Allah, and do neither evil nor
mischief on the (face of the) earth."

Prophet Musa (pbuh) settled with his family in Egypt and decided to confront the king Pharaoh (Firaun) directly, and conveyed to him the message of Allah (SWT), but he laughed and made fun of him. Prophet Musa (pbuh) continued preaching but the Pharaoh and his people were not convinced, so finally in desperation the Prophet Musa (pbuh) said, "O King would you like me to show you that my message is true?" The Pharaoh acknowledged that he would so Prophet Musa (pbuh) performed a miracle by throwing his stick on the ground, which changed into a snake; this miracle shocked the people. Prophet Musa (pbuh) picked up the snake and it returned into its original shape as the stick. Everyone was amazed. Then Prophet Musa (pbuh) put his hand in his armpit and when he took it out his hand was shining with bright light.

In Surah Ash-Shuara C26: V32, Allah (SWT) mentions about the previous miracle that:

"Then he threw down his staff (stick), it was an obvious serpent (snake). And he drew forth his hand and, it appeared white to the beholders."

In another miracle when Firaun's army chased Prophet Musa (pbuh) and his followers, Allah (SWT) revealed the following order to him, as listed in Surah Ash-Shuara C26: V60 that:

"Strike the sea with the rod; and it clove asunder and each part become like a large mountain."

The water of the sea rose up high with a great uproar and the bottom of the sea turned into a dry land. It was an amazing miracle; the people could hardly believe their eyes. The Israelites ran desperately and went far ahead. The Pharaoh (Firaun) and his huge army chased them in hostility. There was a great uproar again and the water from both sides poured and rushed over him and his soldiers. They were completely drowned and Musa (pbuh) and his followers crossed the sea safely.

The Quran explains the above incident in the following surah and how the Pharaoh's army was destroyed:

Surah Ta Ha C20: V90 to V92 - *" And We made the children of Israel to pass through the sea, then Fir'aun and his hosts followed them in hostility and for oppression until when drowning overtook him, he said: I believe that there is no god but He in Whom the children of Israel believe and I am of those who submit. What now! said God, and indeed you have been rebellious and was of the mischief makers. But this day We save you in your body so that you may be a sign to those after you and most surely most people are heedless of Our Signs."*

When Prophet Musa (pbuh) and thousands of his followers destroyed the Pharaoh, they expressed gratitude to Allah (SWT) for his help and mercy. They witnessed a remarkable miracle, and were free to live without any fear and continued to spread Islam across the Arab world for many years.

12.3 Prophet Sulaiman's miracle 'Travelling by Air'

Prophet Sulaiman (pbuh) was the youngest son of Prophet Daud (David) and preached Allah's (SWT) messages about 1,700 years before the birth of Prophet Muhammad (pbuh). Prophet Sulaiman (pbuh) inherited a kingdom from his father and had the ability to communicate with animals, birds and Jinns; he fully understood their language and commanded them.

Once Prophet Sulaiman (pbuh) was travelling through the desert with his army and heard that an ant had warned his fellow ants about the troops heading towards them and who would kill them. Prophet Sulaiman (pbuh) heard the ants' distressed call a few miles away and ordered his army to halt their journey until all the ants crossed safely (Ref: Surah An Naml C27: V17-18).

Prophet Sulaiman (pbuh) was also able to communicate with Jinns and is regarded as their prophet as well; and he regularly instructed them about the one and only Allah. The existence of Jinns is mentioned in the Quran, and they existed before the creation of Adam (pbuh) and were created from smokeless fire. Muslims believe that there are good and evil Jinns; Iblis was a Jinn who disobeyed Allah's (SWT) instructions. All Jinns will be accountable for their deeds as well, just as human beings will.

In the following surah, Allah (SWT) stated that Prophet Sulaiman (pbuh) covered the distance of two months' walk in two strides by flying through the air.

Surah Al Saba C34: V12 - *"And to Solomon (We subjugated) the wind: its morning stride was a month's journey and the evening stride was a month's journey."*

12.4 Miracles performed by Prophet Issa/Jesus (pbuh)

In many verses of the Quran, Allah (SWT) denies the claim of the Christians that He has a son and declares that Prophet Issa (pbuh) (Jesus) was a slave of Allah (SWT) whom he modelled in the womb of his mother like any of his creatures and created him without a father, as he had created Hazrat Adam (pbuh) without a father and mother. All Muslims accepts and believe that Jesus (pbuh) was one of the prophets of Allah (SWT) and is highly respected.

The birth of Prophet Issa (pbuh) itself was a great miracle as his mother Bibi Maryam (Mary), while praying inside a temple received a message from Allah (SWT) through an angel informing her about the birth of her son Prophet Issa (pbuh). The angel said, "I am only a messenger from your Lord to inform you about the gift of an honourable son." In the following surahs, Allah (SWT) informs us about the birth of Prophet Jesus (pbuh):

Surah Al Imran C3: V45 - *Behold! the angels said: "O Mary! Allah giveth thee glad tidings of a Word from Him: his name will be Christ Jesus, the son of Mary, held in honor in this world and the Hereafter and of (the company of) those nearest to Allah."*

Surah Al Imran C3: V46 - *"He shall speak to the people in childhood and in maturity. And he shall be (of the company) of the righteous."*

Surah Al Imran C3: V47 - *She said: "O my Lord! How shall I have a son when no man hath touched me?" He said: "Even so: Allah createth what He willeth: When He hath decreed a plan, He but saith to it, 'Be,' and it is!"*

As Prophet Issa (pbuh) grew, the signs of prophet hood also began to show and increased. He could tell his friends what they had eaten, and what they had hidden and where. During his mission, Prophet Issa (pbuh) performed many other miracles.

In the following surah, Allah (SWT) tells us about the relevant miracles associated with Prophet Issa/Jesus (pbuh):

Surah Al-Imran C3: V49 - *Say Issa that "I have come to you with a sign from your Lord. I make for you the shape of a bird out of clay, I breathe into it, and it becomes a bird by God's permission. I heal the blind from birth and the leper. And I bring the dead to life by God's permission. And I tell you what you eat and what you store in your houses...."*

Muslims believe that Prophet Issa/Jesus (pbuh) was not the son of God nor he was crucified as acclaimed by Christians. It was the plan of his enemies to crucify him, but Allah (SWT) saved him and raised him up (alive) to Him. The likeness of Issa (pbuh) was put onto another man, and his enemies crucified him, thinking that he was Prophet Issa (pbuh). Prophet Issa/Jesus never claimed that he was God. Allah (SWT) says in the Surah An - Nisa C4: V157 that:

...They said, "We killed the Messiah Jesus, son of Mary, the messenger of God. They did not kill him, nor did they crucify him, but the likeness of him was put on another man (and they killed that man)..."

12.5 Miracles performed by Prophet Muhammad (pbuh)

In Islamic history, Prophet Muhammad (pbuh) played a very significant role and started to preach Allah's (SWT) messages in Mecca when the unbelievers dominated and openly rejected the existence of Allah (God) and created many obstacles for those people who believed in one God. Prophet Muhammad (pbuh) persuaded people through his honesty, love, devotion and total faith, rather than performing miracles to convince unbelievers about the one and only Allah (SWT).

Prophet Muhammad (pbuh) continued his total belief in Allah (SWT) and prayed with commitment and passion. A revelation from Allah (SWT) started at the age of 40 when one day while praying inside a cave in the mountain Hira, the Angel Gabriel (Jibrail) appeared and said: "Read." However, Prophet Muhammad (pbuh) was illiterate and could not read or write, so he said to the angel, "I can not read." The angel held Prophet Muhammad (pbuh) and squeezed him as much as he could bear and said again, "Read." Then Prophet Muhammad (pbuh) repeated, "I cannot read", so the angel again squeezed the prophet and said:

"Read! In the name of Your Lord, Who has created (all that exists), has created a man from a clot (a piece of thick coagulated blood). Read! And your Lord is the Most Generous, Who has taught (the writing) by the pen, has taught man that which he knew not."
(Ref: Surah Al - Alaq C96: V1 to V4).

Prophet Muhammad (pbuh) repeated the words and a new mission started, and subsequently many revelations were delivered by Angel Jibrail and later collated into the holy book of Quran. After 1400 years all words of the Quran are original, unchanged and will not be altered. This is why the Quran is a unique book in the form of Allah's (SWT) messages and teachings for all human beings. The most significant and remarkable miracle performed by Allah (SWT) was in the formation of the Quran, as Prophet Muhammad was chosen and honoured for this task. Because of the revelations and Prophet Muhammad's (pbuh) devotion, passion and love for Allah (SWT) Islam flourished and spread throughout the Arab world. In the following surahs, Allah (SWT) informs us about the Quran and its importance:

Surah Yusuf - C12: V2 - *"We have sent it down as an Arabic Qur'an, in order that ye may learn wisdom."*

Surah Al Isra - C17: V88 - Say: *"If the whole of mankind and Jinns were to gather, together to produce the like of this Qur'an, they could not produce the like thereof, even if they backed up each other with help and support."*

The second most unbelievable miracle took place and was performed with the help of Allah (SWT) when Prophet Muhammad (pbuh) was blessed to travel to Al-Miraj. These miracles are also known as Al-Isra and Al-Miraj. In Surah Al Isra C17: V1, Allah (SWT) mentions the Al-Miraj journey:

"Glory to (Allah) Who did take His servant (Muhammad) for a journey by night from the Masjid Al-Haram to Masjid Al-Aqsa, whose precincts We did bless, - in order that We might show him some of Our Signs: for He is the One Who heareth and seeth (all things)."

Before the prophet took his night journey to Al Miraj, the ceiling of the house in which he was staying opened and Angel Jibrail descended. He cut open the chest of Prophet Muhammad (pbuh) and washed the open area with Zumzum (holy) water. Then he emptied something from a container into the chest of the Prophet to increase his wisdom as well as the strength of his belief. This was done to prepare the messenger of Allah (SWT) for what he had yet to see in the upper world among the wonders of the creation of Allah (SWT).

After the ablution, Angel Jibrail came with the Burrak (a white flying horse from paradise) and took Prophet Muhammad (pbuh) first towards Masjid Al-Aqsa, where he prayed salah in the presence of the other prominent prophets. He then untied the Burrak and went up towards the sky, where he first met the Prophet Adam (pbuh), and thereafter advanced towards the second sky, where he met Prophet Yahya (pbuh), to the third sky where he met Prophet Yusuf (pbuh), to the fourth where he met Prophet Idrees (pbuh), the fifth sky where he met Prophet Haroon (pbuh), to the sixth shy, where he met Prophet Musa (pbuh) and in the seventh sky, where he met Prophet Ibrahim. The Prophet Muhammad was also shown hell and heaven and then taken towards 'Sidratul Muntaha' (a tree which nobody besides the Prophet Muhammed (pbuh) was allowed to pass).

Here the prophet (pbuh) saw Allah with his own eyes and salah was made compulsory. He came down and was stopped by Prophet Musa (pbuh) and asked what Allah (SWT) had made compulsory on your 'Ummah' (humankind). The Prophet Muhammad (pbuh) replied "50 salahs", oh Musa' Hazrat Musa (pbuh) told Prophet Muhammad to return and ask Allah (SWT) to decrease the number, because he had tested his Ummah and they could not pray that many salahs. The Prophet Muhammad (pbuh) returned to Allah a few times and finally the number was reduced to five times a day. This is now obligatory for all Muslims.

Prophet Muhammad (pbuh) returned to Mecca where he had left for his journey to Miraj. He returned to the water used for ablution and noticed it was still hot, which was a sign that this journey of thousands and millions of miles took place instantly and must have been faster than the speed of light.

In addition to the above unbelievable miracle, Prophet Muhammad (pbuh) performed other miracles as briefly mentioned in the Sahih Al Bukhari (Hadith):

- On one occasion the unbelievers in Mecca asked Prophet Muhammad (pbuh) to show them a miracle; he showed them the splitting of the moon. (Narrated in Sahih Al Bukhari).

- Another miracle was the flowing of the water through Prophet Muhammad's fingers; when his companions got thirsty and had no water except a little in a vessel, they came to him and told him that they had no water to drink except for what was in the vessel. Prophet Muhammad (pbuh) put his hand in the vessel and the water started gushing out between his fingers, and about one thousand five hundred companions drank the water. (Narrated in Sahih Al Bukhari).

In Surah Al Anaam C6: V101 it is stated that:
"He (Allah) is the originator of heavens and the earth"

13
Some useful facts about the Kaaba

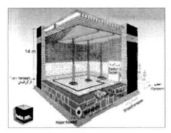

Inside the Kaaba

In Surah Baqara C2: V127 - *it is stated that: "And remember Abraham and Isma'il raised the foundations of the House (With this prayer): 'Our Lord! Accept (this service) from us'..."*

Surah Baqara C2: V144 - *"... and ye (O Muslims), wheresoever ye may be, turn your faces (when ye pray) toward it (Kaaba)..."*

- The Kaaba is located (inside the grand mosque) in the city of Mecca about 70 km from Jeddah-Saudi Arabia.

- The Kaaba is a building (Kibla/direction) towards which Muslims face five times a day, every-day in their prayer.

- According to Islamic tradition and history, Prophet Adam (pbuh) was the first who built the Kaaba for all humanity.

- Prophet Ibrahim (pbuh) and his son Ismail (pbuh) later rebuilt the Kaaba (on the same place) as Allah's house.

- The scholars and historians stated that the Kaaba has been reconstructed between five and twelve times.

- The current height of the Kaaba is about 40 feet (12m) and total area comes to about 1290 square feet (119 sq metres).

- The Kaaba is located in the middle of the Masjid-ul-Haram and its black cover is replaced once a year during the Hajj.

- There are five main gates of Masjid-ul-Haram (Mecca) namely Bab-e-Malik Abdul Aziz, Bab-e-Fateh, Bab-e-Safa, Bab-e-Umrah and Bab-e-Fahad.

- The total area of the Masjid-ul-Haram is about 365,000 sq metres. The capacity for worshippers is up to 1,000,000.

- The inside area of the Kaaba is about 43 x 30 feet (13x9m).

- The Kaaba door is opened twice a year for a ceremony known as 'the cleaning of the 'Kaaba'. This ceremony takes place about fifteen days before the start of Ramadan and the same period before the annual pilgrimage of Hajj.

- Inside the Kaaba there is a marble floor. The interior walls are clad with marble and decorated with Quranic inscriptions.

- The top part of the wall is covered with a green cloth decorated with gold embroidered Quranic verses.

- Lamps hang from a cross beam; there is also a small table for incense burners. The building is otherwise empty.

- One historian counted the total stones/blocks of the Kaaba and found there to be 1,614 and in different shapes.

- In addition, Masjid-ul-haram have the following:
  - there are 4 large domes and 48 small domes.
  - there are a total of 95 gates of the Masjid-ul-Haram
  - there are 9 minarets and there height is 92 metres.

Hajar- ra - Aswad (the black stone)

14
Islam and Sufism

Sufism (or Tasawwuf) is a mystical belief and practice in which Muslims seek to find the truth of divine love and knowledge through direct pray and personal experience with Almighty God (Allah). It consists of variety of mystical paths and concepts that are designed to ascertain the nature of man and God, and to facilitate the experience of the presence of divine love and wisdom in the world. A practitioner of this tradition is known as Sufi (Dervish or Wali). Ibn Khaldun, the 14th century Arab historian, described Sufism as "... dedicated to worship, total dedication to Allah, disregard for the finery and ornament of the world, abstinence from the pleasure, wealth, and prestige sought by most men, and retiring from others to worship alone". Non-Muslims often mistake Sufism as a sect of Islam. Through the centuries, Sufis contributed hugely to Islamic literature. For example, Rumi, Omar Khayyám and Al-Ghazali's influence extended beyond Muslim lands to be quoted by Western philosophers, writers and theologians.

After the death of last and final Prophet Muhammad (pbuh) and his companions (Suhabas), Islam flourished through Arab world, SE Asia, Far East, Africa, Europe, and other parts of the world. All famous Imams and Sufis led a simple life and thoroughly read the Quran with meanings, strictly followed its ethics and conveyed the true messages of Islam in their special ways, and converted millions of non-believers into Islam through love, peace and harmony. In this respect Imams Hanifa, Shafi, Malik, Hanbal and Jaffar are well respected, recognised and hold a special place in Islam along with other great Sufis, and their contributions certainly helped to spread Islam across the Indian subcontinent and other parts of the world.

The Sufi movement has spanned several continents and cultures over a millennium, at first expressed through Arabic, then through Persian, Turkish and many other languages. Both Sunni and Shia

---

doctrine practice Sufism in their special way. As the Sufism became popular, various Ulma (Scholars) voiced their opinions by contradicting each other and supporting their respective ideology. There are three prime schools of thought, which represent various scholars' views. First, the conformists say that there are no surahs and authentic hadiths, which directly support or encourage Sufism. The second belief advocate that the need to learn from a teacher is based on the Quranic verses C16: V43 and C31: V15 and it states that *"Ask those who know if you know not"* and *"And follow the path of him who turns unto me (Allah)"*. Finally, the moderate adherents say that there is no harm visiting Sufis' shrines and paying tribute to them, reciting Quran or praying for their forgiveness, as long as no shirk is committed and Islamic ethics are maintained throughout.

Following Sufism is a personal choice, therefore, must not be influenced or opposed, as there is no compulsion in Islam and nobody should be forced to do against his or her desire.

The following is a brief list of the prominent Sufis:

Hazrat Jalaaluddin Muhammad Rumi (1207 - 1273 CE), was a 13th century Persian poet, jurist, theologian and Sufi mystic.

Hazrat Sheikh Abdul Qadir Gilani (1077 - 1166 CE), was a Persian Hanbali preacher, Sufi, Sheikh and head of the Qadri Sufi order.

Hazrat Khwaja Moiuddin Chishti (1141 - 1230 CE), was a most famous Persian Sufi and saint of the Chishti order. He preached throughout the subcontinent and his shrine is in Ajmer - India.

Hazrat Baba Bulleh (Abdullah) Shah (1680 - 1757 CE), was a Sufi and poet born in Bahawalpur. His shrine is in Kasur - Pakistan.

Hazrat Fariduddin Gunj Shakar was a 12th century Sufi preacher and saint born in Multan and his shrine is in Pak Patan - Pakistan.

Hazrat Ali Hujwari Gunj Bukish (around 990 CE), born in Ghazni, Afghanistan. He was a great Sufi and scholar, and significantly contributed in spreading Islam in South Asia. His shrine is located in Lahore - Pakistan, where millions of people pay tribute to him.

15
Why there are misconceptions about Islam and its followers

Regrettably, Islam is perceived in Europe and North America as a controversial religion, and its principles are often reported in a negative manner by the anti-Islamic media and critics. It appears that they look for every opportunity to paint a dark picture of Islam and its followers. Why - have we (collectively) analysed the main factors that generate such negative publicity and animosity in the world about Islam? It is important that we first impartially review the relevant reasons before advocating narrow-minded and unilateral conclusions that would have an adverse effect on unbelievers and followers of Islam. In order to clarify any delusion, we must also examine why anti-Islamic feelings are initiated in the first place and what can be done to tackle such conflicts and ensure that correct messages are relayed to eradicate myths about Islam.

In the author's opinion, ignorance, poverty, injustice, lack of mutual respect, ambiguous teachings and not fully understanding the Islamic ethics are some of the major contributory factors, which create confusion, friction and mistrust among different faiths. It is also noted that after the 11/9/01 (US) and 7/7/05 (UK) incidents which vast majority of Muslims condemned, but regrettably, such appalling acts initiated a 'them and us' division and anti-Muslim propaganda against Islam. As a result, many people in the un-Islamic world think that majority of Muslims are extremist and their religion is based on prejudice. It is also widely believed that Muslims dislike western values and are threat to civilization. This notion is obviously fictitious, as Islam promotes democracy and prohibits suicide attacks, terrorising and killing of innocent people. Unfortunately, many unjust myths and conspiracy theories from both sides are based on ignorance, and failed to establish the root causes, which encourage radical activities, animosity and mistrust.

In this section, the author addresses both Muslims and non-Muslims and identifies some of the main reasons, which initiate clash of ideologies and radicalism. The following major root causes apply to all communities and incite sensitive religious, social and political issues, and create animosity among diverse faiths. The facts are that:

- There is a lack of unity, leadership and co-ordination between Muslim Ulma and people when dealing with the core religious, social and cultural issues. For example, every year religious festivals are celebrated in the UK on different days because of a lack of consensus about new month's moon sighting and date.

- In a majority of cases the Quran is taught without its meanings and, as a result, adults and children do not fully understand its exact messages and fail to apply them correctly in their daily life.

- In a tiny minority of cases radical ideas are promoted and, as a result, some people are misled and brainwashed, and try to force their extremist views on fellow Muslims and other believers.

- Different Muslim scholars and politicians voice their opinions in a contradictory manner, which confuses the issues and, as a result, both electronic and print media of the non-Muslim world take full advantage and publicise negative events.

- There is a lack of understanding of Islam and other cultures. In addition, evidence of high unemployment, loneliness, injustice and oppression of Muslims is apparent in some part of the world.

- Ambiguous and double standards are adopted by the world's leaders and well publicised ill-treatment and repression of the Muslims in various parts of the world plays a major part when dealing with religious, political and social issues. Naturally, these factors create frustration, revulsion and resentment against the aggressor (only a tiny minority of radical minded people think this way). Leading politicians and governments must also accept that until religious, political, humanitarian and territorial conflicts relating to Muslims are resolved with bilateral consent, a long-lasting peace is unlikely to be achieved in the world.

- Not many politicians and religious leaders/scholars (Ulma) try to defuse the friction between Muslims and other communities. Everybody thinks that their religion and culture is superior to others and often there is a 'them and us' attitude and barriers are erected for personal or political reasons, which creates conflicts.

- There is a lack of tolerance and ignorance about various faiths and cultures. In a majority of cases, prejudiced teachings and individual religious sects are promoted (instead of the teachings of the Quran and Sunnah), which creates obstacles to restore trust, peace and harmony. This is a joint duty of the politicians and religious scholars to reduce hatred for the sake of humanity.

- Arrogance, dictatorial attitudes and biased policies pursued by some of the superpowers and their allies (after 9/11 and 7/7) against the Muslim countries initiate resentment, distrust and sense of revenge. As a result, many anti-Western opponents take full advantage and radicalise young Muslims across the world.

- There is no or little interaction and reluctance among diverse societies, which prevent them to become close to each other.

- Various anti-Islamic agents often issue offensive statements as part of the 'freedom of speech' policy to demean Muslims, and such foolish acts instigate religious unrest and backlash.

Interfaith dialogue: the way forward

It is the responsibility of all Muslims (regardless of their heritage or personal belief) to promote authentic Islamic and the Quran's teachings in its true light without any personal, financial or political motives. Muslims must also agree and establish common goals by avoiding contradictions, making controversial statements and being intolerant or unfriendly. This can be achieved by showing unity and celebrating various religious festivals (such as Ramadan, Eid-ul-Fither, etc) on one day with bilateral consent and dialogue with the community. This applies to all sects of the religion and suggests that there is an urgency and need for all of us to resolve our religious and cultural affairs first before criticising others or being pessimistic.

It is quite possible that Muslims will encounter some incidents, when unbelievers will try to provoke and make silly comments about Islam and its followers. The examples of Charles Darwin's 1859 controversial theory of evolution and the 1927 Big Bang theory of the Belgian priest Georges Lemaitre are typical cases usually raised by unbelievers. In such cases the best way is to be calm, listen to them first and try to understand their views and how they perceive Islam; be tolerant and try to answer them with historical facts. Also, mention the relevant quotations from the Quran, which revealed scientific facts about the creation of universe and humanity over 1400 years ago, as opposed to being discovered by human during the last 100 years or so. The factual and logical reply to divisive theories and misconceptions will encourage you to discuss other issues more openly and assertively with authority.

In addition, discuss and put your views in an intellectual and persuasive manner, as these will be your strong points against any unbeliever. Do not try to be arrogant or force your personal views onto others, as this will give a wrong impression about Islam and its followers. Muslims must also try their utmost best to reject old un-Islamic cultural and regional customs that have been adopted from the unbelievers many centuries ago, which are not based on Islamic principles and teachings. Try to read the Quran with its meanings, understand and try to act upon it and follow the teachings of Islam as being a kind, tolerant and peaceful religion, and spread love and harmony to all humanity. This is one of many strengths of Islam, which has been misinterpreted, misunderstood and unfortunately incorrectly conveyed to other communities.

Do not hesitate to express your views and openly condemn any wrongdoing in a peaceful manner (i.e. things not allowed in Islam such as suicide attacks, terrorising and killing of innocent people, etc.) and remarks often made by critics of Islam. Do not support extremist or radical groups, which promote violence and reject their ideologies, personal and narrow views. You will only be able to promote Islam in its true light if your personal knowledge is thorough and based on authentic Islamic teachings and practices.

The following key notes apply to all communities and groups, and require further attention to ease friction, animosity and mistrust. This will help to maintain social cohesion among diverse faiths:

- Try to listen and respect other people's views. Be calm, tolerant and do not become highly emotional or aggressive.

- Be aware of anti-Islamic propaganda and act wisely.

- Do not follow speculations and impose your personal views on other people, as this is against Islam and will backfire.

- Put your views and ideas positively, intellectually and in a persuasive manner with logical and practical examples.

- Read the Quran with meanings, understand and practice its main ethics, and try to convey the true messages of Islam as being a kind, tolerant and peaceful religion.

- All communities must try their best to integrate with local people and must show their loyalty to their chosen country of residence and endorse peace, tolerance and mutual respect.

- It is the responsibility of the religious teachers and parents to educate their children about true Islam and its teachings, and must encourage them to read the Quran with meanings.

- In order to tackle ignorance about Islam, mistrust and lack of mutual respect amongst diverse communities, it is important that local authorities promote interfaith dialogues, interaction and introduce awareness and trust-building workshops.

- Governments in power should do more, and provide facilities and job opportunities for Muslims without any discrimination.

- The media and critics of Islam must act responsibly and avoid inciting sensitive issues, as biased views initiate resistance.

- In order to maintain an enduring peace, all leading politicians must review their respective country's foreign policy and the double standards being applied against Muslims, and establish the root causes and preventative actions required to resolve the current international political and territorial conflicts.

16
The Message

The following is the salient message that the Prophet Muhammad (pbuh) eloquently conveyed and left for Muslims during his Hajj pilgrimage at the Mount Arafat (632 CE) stating that:

"I have left two things among you, and you will not stray as long as you hold them strongly; one is the Book of Allah (the Quran), the other the laws of His Messenger (Sunnah)" (Narrated in Sahih Al-Bukhari and Al-Muslim)

In the Quran, Allah (SWT) clearly instructs all humankind about his existence, the ultimate powers he possesses, the things he provides, life after death, judgment day and reminds everyone about the rewards in heaven and severe punishments in hell, etc. All this was revealed over 1400 years ago for the sake of humanity, so that we could take note of Allah's instructions and be able to distinguish between good and bad, and follow his messages with total sincerity, love and passion without any influence or fear. This is one way to be close to Allah (SWT) and be his servant.

There are many misconceptions perceived in the public about Islam, and one of them is that those Muslims who grow or keep a beard, wear non-Western clothes, caps, hajab or veil are better and more religious than those who do not follow the Islamic dress code. This fallacy is widely advocated by some of the religious clerics and regarded as an obligatory duty. In reality, wearing Islamic clothes is a personal choice and there is no compulsion. This creates a stereotyped impression within society, and such people are often unjustly labelled as being 'orthodox or extremist'. As a result, some people in the West believe that Islam is a strict religion and that the majority of its followers do not integrate with the local community.

What is the point of praying five times a day and yet not observing other basic requirements of Islam? What is the use of reading the Quran in the Arabic language and not understanding its meanings? What really matters are the inner feelings, sincere intentions, understanding the religious obligations, and more importantly acting upon and following all mandatory duties, as mentioned in the Quran and Hadith (Sunnah) with commitment, love and passion. Islam is a peaceful and flexible religion and must therefore be practiced with open mind, without compromising or giving up any of the Islamic principles or being influenced by other people's personal views and controversial philosophies.

As mentioned before, the main purpose of writing this book is to clarify unjust misconceptions about Islam, building a solid foundation for further study and deeper understanding of Islamic ethics. How interfaith dialogue, mutual respect and tolerance can help to bring different communities close to each other? What are the main duties of Muslims and the best way to comprehend and accomplish them? How Muslims can fulfil their duties within a busy lifestyle? In author's experience, Muslims can follow their obligations wherever they live providing that they make sincere efforts, devote some time and keep religious, social and political issues separate. Muslims must not allow anyone to impose their personal or radicalised views on them; you make an independent study and analysis of the Quran, decide which mandatory duty you could follow within your lifestyle and leave the rest to Allah (SWT). As he is the most merciful, and final judge of all human beings good and bad deeds and will reward everyone accordingly.

"There is no compulsion in religion..." (Ref: Al Quran C2:V256)

The following is a summary of obligatory duties for Muslims, which must be pursued at all times, and remember that there are no short cuts to paradise; only sincere and good deeds will help you to become a good Muslim and could earn you a place in heaven.

- All Muslims must truly believe and accept that there is only one God (Allah) and nobody else is worthy of worship. Prophet Muhammad (pbuh) is the last and final Rasool, Nabi and messenger of Allah, and this belief must be followed sincerely.

- Muslims must try their best and follow all pillars and beliefs of Islam and guidelines of the Quran. Read the Quran in your native and commanding language with meanings, and follow its messages in real life with sincere efforts and passion.

- Muslims must also follow the Sunnah's (Hadith) guidelines and respect other religions. Be honest and tolerant, kind to all human beings, be grateful to Allah (SWT) for his kindness and mercy, and look after your parents, family and poor people.

- As a Muslim, try to convey the true messages of the Quran to all communities and openly promote love, peace, mutual respect and harmony message to all human beings (regardless of their religion, colour or race), together with main attributes of Islam.

In addition, it is the responsibility of the parents to teach their children about authentic Islamic ethics and encourage them to read the Quran with meanings, so that they fully understand and apply its main messages in their lives without any fear. Children must also be taught to respect all religions, be restrained and follow the laws of the resident country and try to be a good citizen.

May Allah (SWT) guide all of us, accept our sincere efforts and prayers, and make this world a peaceful place where all human beings can live together with love and harmony - Ameen!

"Any other religion other than ISLAM will not be acceptable to me..." (Ref: Al Quran C3:V85)

"Allah will not forgive anyone who creates his associates and pray to other than him..." (Ref: Al Quran C4:V48 & V116)

"All human beings are equal, nobody is superior to other except by good deeds and good actions. (Regardless of their race, gender, nationality, wealth or social status.)"
(Narrated in Sahih Al Bukhari and Al Muslim)

Appendix A
The 99 beautiful names of Allah (SWT)

In the following surahs, Allah (SWT) informs us that:

Surah Al Araf - C7: V180 - *"The most beautiful names belong to God: so call on Him by the..."*

Surah Al Hashr - C59: V24 - *"He is Allah, the Creator, the Evolver, the Bestower of Forms. To Him belong the Most Beautiful Names: whatever is in the heavens and on earth, all declare His Praises and Glorifies Him: and He is the Almighty, the Wise."*

The 99 names are also known as the major attributes of Allah, and all Muslims are urged to remember them with their meanings.

The 99 most beautiful names of Allah (SWT) together with his attributes and brief explanation are listed below together with a brief cross-reference to each surah/verse/ayah in which Allah's (SWT) attributes relates to are mentioned (it is quite possible that the same attribute may appear in other surahs):

1. Allah (in Arabic)

2. Ar-Rahmaan
The Compassionate
(Surah Ar - Rahmaan C56:1-13)

3. Ar-Raheem
The Most Merciful
(Surah Fatihah C1:1-3)

4. Al-Mailk
The Absolute Ruler
(Surah Ta Ha C20:113-114)

5. Al Quddus
The Holy (Pure)
(Surah Al Baqara C2:252)

6. As-Salam
The Source of Peace
(Surah Yunus C10:25)

7. Al-Mu'min
The Guardian of Faith
(Surah Al Ahazab C33:41)

8. Al-Muhaymin
The Protector
(Surah Al Maidah C5:48)

9. Al-'Aziz
The Victorious
(Surah Al-Fath C48:7)

10. Al-Jabbar
The Compeller
(Surah Ibrahim C14:15)

11. Al-Mutakabbir
The Greatest
(Surah Luqman C31:30)

12. Al-Khaliq
The Creator
(Surah AlHashr C59:24)

13. Al-Bari'
The Maker of Order
(Surah Al-Furqan C25:2)

14. Al-Musawwir
The Shaper of Beauty
(Surah Al-Baqara C2:29)

15. Al-Ghaffar
The Forgiving
(Surah Al-Buruj C85:14-16)

16. Al-Qahhar
The Dominant
(Surah Yusuf C12:39)

17. Al-Wahhab
The Giver of All
(Surah Ash-Shu'ara C26:21)

18. Ar Razaaq
The Sustainer
(Surah Ghafir C40:64)

19. Al-Fattah
The Opener
(Surah Al-A'raf C7:89)

20. Al-'Alim
The Knower of All
(Surah As-Sajdah C32:6-7)

21. Al-Qabid
The Retainer
(Surah Al-Furqan C25:45)

22. Al-Basit
The Expender
(Surah Ash-Sharh C94)

23. Al-Khafid
The Abaser
(Surah Al-Waqi'ah C56:103)

24. Ar-Rafi'
The Exalter
(Surah Ghafir C40:15-16)

25. Al-Mu'izz
The Bestower of Honors
(Surah An-Nisa C4:139)

26. Al-Mudhill
The Humiliator
(Surah At-Tawbah C9:2)

27. As-Sami
The Hearer of All
(Surah Al-Baqarah C2:224)

28. Al-Basir
The Seer of All
(Surah Al 'Imran C3:15)

29. Al-Hakam
The Judge
(Surah An-Nisa C4:58)

30. Al Adil
The Just
(Surah An-Nahl C16:90)

31. Al-Lateef
The Subtle One
(Surah Al-An'am C6:101-3)

32. Al-Khabir
The All-Aware
(Surah Al-Mulk C67:14)

33. Al-Haleem
The Forbearing
(Surah Al-Baqara C2:263)

34. Al Azeem
The Magnificent
(Surah Ash-Shura C42:4)

35. Al-Ghafur
The Forgiver
(Surah Al-Baqara C2:58)

36. Ash-Shakur
The Rewarder
(Surah An-Naml C27:40)

37. Al-'Ali
The Highest
(Surah Ash-Shura C42:2)

38. Al-Kabir
The Greatest
(Surah Al-Hajj C22:62)

39. Al-Hafiz
The Preserver
(Surah Qaf C50:4)

40. Al-Muqit
The Guardian
(Surah Fussilat C41:10)

41. Al-Hasib
The one who gives satisfaction
(Surah An-Nisa C4:86)

42. Al-Jaleel
The Mighty
(Surah Ar-Rahman C55:78)

43. Al-Kareem
The Generous
(Surah Al-Hadid C57:12)

---

44. Ar-Raqeeb
The Watchful One
(Surah Qaf C50:16-18)

45. Al-Mujeeb
The Responder
(Surah Hud C11:61)

46. Al-Wasi'
The Knowledgable
(Surah Al-A'raf C7:89)

47. Al-Hakeem
The Perfectly Wise
(Surah An-Naml C27:6)

48. Al-Wadud
The Loving One
(Surah Al-Buruj C85:14)

49. Al-Majeed
The Majestic One
(Surah Ar-Rahman C55:26)

50. Al-Ba'ith
The Resurrector
(Surah Al-Hajj C22:5-6)

51. Ash-Shahid
The Witness
(Surah An-Nisa C4:166)

52. Al-Haqq
The Truth
(Surah Al-An'am C6:102)

53. Al-Wakil
The Trustee
(Surah Al-An'am C6:102)

54. Al-Qawi
One with complete power
(Surah Ash-Shura C42:19)

55. Al-Matin
The Forceful One
(Surah Al-A'raf C7)

56. Al-Wali
The Governor
(Surah Ar-Ra'd C13:2)

57. Al-Hameed
The Praised One
(Surah Ash-Shura 42:28)

58. Al-Muhsi
The Appraiser
(Surah Az-Zumar 39:34-35)

59. Al-Mubdi
The Originator
(Surah An-Naml 27:64)

60. Al-Mu'id
The Restorer
(Surah Saba C34:49)

61. Al-Muhyi
The Giver of Life
(Surah Ar-Rum C30:50)

62. Al-Mumit
The Taker of Life
(Surah Al-Mu'minun C23:80)

63. Al-Hayy
The Ever Living One
(Surah Al-Imran C3:1)

64. Al-Qayyum
The Self-Existing One
(Surah Al 'Imran C3:2)

---

65. Al-Waajid
The Finder
(Surah Ad-Duha C93:6-7)

66. Al-Maajid
The Glorious
(Surah Al-Buruj C85:14-15)

67. Al-Wahid
The Only One
(Surah Al-Muddaththir 74:11)

68. As-Samad
The Satisfier of All Needs
(Surah Al-Ikhlas C112)

69. Al-Qadir
The Most Powerful
(Surah Al-Ma'idah C5:17)

70. Al-Muqtadir
The Creator of All Power
(Surah Al-Kahf C18:45)

71. Al- Muqaddim
The Expediter
(Surah Yunus C10:11)

72. Al-Mu'akhkhir
The Delayer
(Surah An-Nahl C16:61)

73. Al-Awwal
The First
(Surah Al-Qasas C28:69-70)

74. Al-Akhir
The Last
(Surah Al-Hadid C57:3)

75. Az-Zahir
The Manifest - Victorious
(Surah Al-Hadid C57:7)

76. Al-Batin
The Hidden One
(Surah Al Hadid C57:3)

77. Al-Walee
The Protecting Friend
(Surah Al-Jathiyah C45:19)

78. Al-Muta'ali
The Supreme One
(Surah Ar-Ra'd C13:9)

79. Al-Barr
The Doer of Good
(Surah Al-An'am C6:97)

80. At-Tawwab
The Guide to Repentance
(Surah At-Tawbah C9:104)

81. Al- Muntaqim
The Avenger
(Surah Zukhruf C43:40-42)

82. Al-'Afu
The Forgiver
(Surah An-Najm C53:32)

83. Ar-Ra'uf
The Clement
(Surah Al-Ma'idah C5:101)

84. Malik ul-Mulk
The Owner of All
(Surah Ya Sin C36:83)

85. Dhul-Jalali Wal-Ikram
The Lord of Majesty/Bounty
(Surah Ar-Rahman C55:26-27)

86. Al-Muqsit
The Equitable One
(Surah Al-Ma'idah C5:42)

87. Al-Jami'
The Gatherer
(Surah Ash-Shura C42:29)

88. Al-Ghani
The Rich One Harm
(Surah Al-Hajj C22:64)

89. Al-Mughni
The Enricher
(Surah An-Najm 53:49-50)

90. Al-Maani'
The Preventer of
(Surah Al-Jinn C72:26-28)

91. Ad-Daarr
The Creator of the Harmful
(Surah Hud C11:9-11)

92. An-Nafi'
The Creator of Good
(Surah Ar-Rum 30:37)

93. An-Nour
The Light
(Surah An-Nur 24:35)

94. Al-Hadi
The Guide
(Surah An-Naml 27:63)

95. Al-Badi'
The Originator
(Surah Al-Ankabut C29:20)

96. Al-Baqi
The Everlasting One
(Surah Ta-Ha C20:73)

97. Al-Warith
The Inheritor of All
(Surah Maryam C19:40)

98. Ar-Rasheed
The Righteous Teacher
(Surah Al-A'la C87:7-8)

99. As- Sabur
The Patient One
(Surah Al-Anfal C8:46)

The most beautiful
name of Allah (SWT)
(2,698 times listed in the Quran)

In Surah Bani Israil C17: V110 it is stated that:

"Call upon Allah or call upon Rahman:
by whatever name ye call upon Him (it is the same). His
are the Most Beautiful Names."

Also, in Surah Ta-Ha C20: V8 it is mentioned that:

"Allah! there is no god but He!
To Him belong the Most Beautiful Names."

Appendix B
Prominent angels and their duties as mentioned in the Quran and Hadith

In Surah Al Anbiya C21: V27, Allah (SWT) states that:

"They (angels) are but honored servants; they speak not until He has spoken; and they act by His (Allah's) command."

According to hadiths, Allah (SWT) created unknown angels from light before the creation of human beings in the form of Prophet Adam (pbuh). All angels are obedient servants and perform their specific duties day and night as commanded by Allah. There are four angels' names mentioned in the Quran (Angel Jibrail, Meekail, Haroot and Maroot). In the hadith, Sahih Al-Bukhari and Sahih Al-Muslim other prominent angels' names are stated, and their duties are briefly highlighted as follows together with the angels' names:

- **Angel Jibrail** (pbuh) was responsible for conveying messages of Allah (SWT) to various prophets as instructed by him.
- **Angel Meekail** (pbuh) is responsible for bringing thunder and lighting onto earth as instructed by Allah (SWT).
- **Angel Izraeel** (pbuh) is known as 'Angel of Death'.
- **Angel Israfeel** (pbuh) will blow the trumpet on the day of the final judgment day as per Allah's (SWT) instructions.
- **Angel Ridwan** (pbuh) is the angel who is responsible for Heaven.
- **Angel Maalik** (pbuh) is the chief of angels who guards Hell.
- **Angels Munkir and Nakir** (pbut) - After death, these two angels question souls in the grave about their religion and faith.
- **Angels Kiraamun Kaatibeen** (pbut) are the two angels who record the good and bad deeds of all human beings (what they do or did during their lifetime) for the final judgment day.

Appendix C
The 25 names of the prophets as mentioned in the Quran

In the holy Quran, Allah (SWT) mentions 25 prominent prophets' names and their attributes. It is obligatory for all Muslims to respect them as part of their belief and religious duty. In Surah Al Imran C3: V84 Allah (SWT) informs us that:

Say: "We believe in Allah and in what has been revealed to us and what was revealed to Ibrahim, Isma`il, Isaac Jacob and the Tribes and in (Books) given to Moses, Jesus and the Prophets from their Lord; we make no distinction between one and another among them and to Allah do we bow our will (in Islam)."

According to a saying of Prophet Muhammad (pbuh), there were about 124,000 prophets/nabis sent to various nations and tribes throughout the history since Allah (SWT) first created Prophet Adam (pbuh) and the last Prophet Muhammad (pbuh). Only 25 names of the Prophets/Nabis have been mentioned in the Quran and their names are listed below in chronological order together with the number of times their names appear in the Quran (listed in bracket against each prophet's name). May Allah's blessings and mercy be upon them all - Ameen!

1. Prophet **Adam** (pbuh) -   (25)

2. Prophet **Idris** (Enoch) (pbuh) -   (2)

3. Prophet **Nuh** (Noah) (pbuh) -   (43)

4. Prophet **Hud** (pbuh) -   (7)

5. Prophet **Saleh** (pbuh) -   (9)

6. Prophet **Lut** (Lot) (pbuh) -   (27)

7.   Prophet **Ibrahim** (Abraham) (pbuh) -   (69)

8.   Prophet **Ismail** (pbuh) -   (12)

9.   Prophet **Isaq** (Issac) (pbuh) -   (17)

10. Prophet **Yaqoob** (Jacob) (pbuh) -   (16)

11. Prophet **Yusuf** (Joseph) (pbuh) -   (27)

12. Prophet **Shuaib** (pbuh) -   (11)

13. Prophet **Haroon** (Aaron) (pbuh) -   (20)

14. Prophet **Musa** (Moses) (pbuh) -   (136)

15. Prophet **Dau'd** (David) (pbuh) -   (16)

16. Prophet **Sulaiman** (Solomon) (pbuh) -   (17)

17. Prophet **Ayyub** (Job) (pbuh) -   (4)

18. Prophet **Dhu'l Kifl** (Ezekiel) (pbuh) -   (2)

19. Prophet **Yunus** (Jonah) (pbuh) -   (4)

20. Prophet **Ilyas** (Elias) (pbuh) -   (3)

21. Prophet **al-Yasa'** (Elisha) (pbuh) -   (2)

22. Prophet **Zakariya** (Zakarias) (pbuh) -   (7)

23. Prophet **Yahya** (John) (pbuh) -   (5)

24. Prophet **Issa** (Jesus) (pbuh) -   (29)

25. Prophet **Muhammad** (pbuh) -   (4)

In Surah Al Mumin C40: V78 it is clearly stated that:
"And certainly We sent messengers before you: there are some of them that We have mentioned to you and there are others whom We have not mentioned to you..."

Appendix D
Some famous messages/hadiths of the last & final Prophet Muhammad (pbuh)

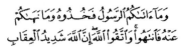

"And whatever the Messenger gives you, take it, and whatever he forbids you, leave it. And fear Allah: truly Allah is severe in punishment." (Ref: Surah Al Hashr C59: V7)

In hadith books (there are six versions, but Sahih Al-Bukhari and Sahih Al-Muslim are known to be the most authentic and popular). There are between 7,000 and 9,000 sayings and actions of Prophet Muhammad (pbuh), and his teachings and messages are known as 'Sunnah'. Both Sahih Bukhari and Sahih Muslim comprehensively covers important religious and social issues such as belief, prayer, fasting, zakat, pilgrimage, ablution, marriage, divorce, commerce, inheritance, crime, punishment, wills, war, food and drink etc. In order to be a 'Good Muslim', all followers are obliged to read the authentic hadiths and try to understand and act upon them.

The following are some of the famous hadiths of last Prophet Muhammad (pbuh) narrated in Al-Bukhari and Al-Muslim stating:

1. I have left two things among you, and you will not stray as long as you hold them strongly; one is the Book of Allah, the other the laws of his Messenger.

2. A true Muslim (Momin) is thankful to Allah in prosperity and resigned to his will in adversity.

3. Heaven/Paradise lies beneath the feet of mothers.

4. He who wishes to enter paradise at the best door must please his parents (both father and mother).

5. A man is bound to do good to his parents, although they may have harmed him or raised their voice.

6. Paradise is nearer to you than the laces of your shoes.

---

7. The best of charity is that which the right hand gives and the left hand does not know about it.

8. Once, Prophet Muhammad (pbuh) was asked what paradise is. He replied, "It is what the eye have not seen, nor the ear heard, nor a mind of a man can imagine."

9. When you see a person who has been given more than you in money and beauty then look to those who have been given less and unfortunate.

10. Look to those inferior to yourselves so that you may not hold Allah's (SWT) benefits in contempt.

11. The greatest crimes/sins are to associate another with Allah (SWT), disobedience to your father and mother, to murder your own species and innocent peoples, to commit suicide and to swear to lie.

12. The grave is the first step of the journey into eternity.

13. Sleep is the brother of death.

14. A martyr shall be pardoned every fault but debt.

15. Every woman who asked to be divorced from her husband without a good cause or reason, the fragrance of the 'Paradise Garden' would be forbidden for her.

16. Once Prophet Muhammad (pbuh) was asked, "What are the duties of Muslims to each other?" He replied, "When you meet a Muslim, greet him, and when he invite you to dinner, accept his invitation; and when he ask you for advice, give it to him; and when he sneeze and say, 'Praise be to Allah,' do you say, 'May Allah have mercy upon thee;' and when he is sick, visit him and when he die follow his bier."

17. Allah's kindness towards his creatures (human beings) is more than a mother's towards her child.

18. Allah is not merciful to who is not kind to mankind.

19. In another occasion, Prophet Muhammad (pbuh) said that guard yourselves from six things, and I am your security for paradise. When you speak, speak the truth; perform when you promise; be trustworthy; be chaste in thought and action; and withhold your hand from striking, and taking or claiming which is unlawful and bad.

20. Those who earn an honest living are close to Allah.

21. Give the labourer his wage before his sweat be dry.

22. Go in quest for knowledge even unto China.

23. Seek knowledge from the cradle to the grave.

24. That person who shall die while he is studying, in order to revive the knowledge of religion, will only be one degree inferior to the prophets.

25. One learned man is harder on the devil than a thousand of ignorant worshippers.

26. The ink of the scholar is more righteous than the blood of the martyr. (This hadith refers to the importance of Dawah).

27. One hour's meditation on the work of the creator is better than seventy years of prayer.

28. Once, Prophet Muhammad was asked, "Who is the best man?" He said, "He is the best man whose life is long and whose actions are good. The worst man is he whose life is long and whose actions are bad."

29. The best of persons in Allah's sight is the best amongst his friends; and the best of neighbours near Allah (SWT) is the best person in his own neighbourhood.

30. Do you love your creator? Love your fellow-human beings first and in return, Allah (SWT) will love you.

31. You do not do evil to those who do evil to you, but you deal with them with forgiveness and kindness.

32. Once, Prophet Muhammad said that I and the guardian of orphans (whether the orphan is of his near or distant relations or of strangers) will be in one place in the paradise like my two fingers, nearly touching each other.

33. The best Muslim house is that in which an orphan, who is well treated, and the worst Muslim house is that in which an orphan is ill-treated.

34. The duty of a junior to a senior brother is as that of a child to its father.

35. A man's first charity should be to his own family, if they are poor and need help.

36. Honestly earned wealth is a blessing and a man may lawfully endeavour to increase it by proper means.

37. He will not enter Paradise who behaved or badly treated his slaves/servants.

38. Feed the hungry and visit a sick person, and free the captive, if he is unjustly confined. Assist any person oppressed, whether Muslim or non-Muslim.

39. He is not of me who, when he speaks, speak falsely; who, when he promises, break his promises; and who, when trust is reposed on him, failed in his trust.

40. The taker of usury/interest and the giver of it, and the writer of its papers and the witness to it, are equal in crime and will be accountable for their deeds.

41. When a woman perform five times of prayer and fast during the month of Ramadan, and is chaste (good character), and is not disobedient to her husband, then tell her to enter paradise by whichever door she likes.

42. The best among you are those who read the Quran, understand and follow its teachings, and convey its messages to other people through Dawah (invitation).

Appendix E
Major sins and crimes in Islam

The major sins and crimes are those acts or behaviours, which are forbidden by Allah (SWT) in the Quran and by his final messenger Muhammad (pbuh) in the hadiths. It is, therefore, the obligatory duty of every Muslim to avoid all sins as listed in this section.

"If you avoid the great (things) which ye are forbidden, We will remit from you your evil deeds and make you enter at a noble gate".
(Ref: Surah Al Nisa C4:V31)

"Surely, Allah will not forgive the Associations with Him, but forgives whomever He wishes..."
(Ref: Surah Al Nisa C4:V48 and V116)

This means that Allah (SWT) will not forgive anybody who creates his associate(s) (Shareek) and prays to other than him. Allah (SWT) is the greatest, the most gracious, merciful, and we should only pray to him for his kindness and forgiveness in all circumstances and difficulties (no matter what happens or whatever the causes are). The following are some of the major (Kabera) sins and crimes, which are identified in the holy book of Quran and authentic hadiths, and all Muslims must try to keep away from them. The list is only compiled for guidance purposes, and its importance or order of listing may vary according to various Ulmas (scholars) or books: May Allah (SWT) protect and forgive us all - Ameen!

1. Creating Allah's (SWT) associate(s)/Shareeks.

2. Murder or killing of innocent people.

3. Practicing black magic and misleading people.

4. Not praying Salah/Namaz every day.

5. Not paying Zakat to poor and needy people.

6. Not fasting during Ramadan without good reasons.

7. Not performing Hajj, while being able to do so.

8. Not respecting parents and looking after them.

9. Committing suicide (under any circumstances).

10. Abandoning relatives and not helping them.

11. Fornication and Adultery.

12. Homosexuality (sodomy).

13. Usury/interest - earning or taking interest on savings.

14. Wrongfully taking the property or money of orphans.

15. Suicide attacks, terrorising people and creating fear.

16. Kidnapping people for personal or political reasons.

17. Drinking alcohol (wine, etc.) and being intoxicated.

18. Pride and arrogance (being proud or showing off).

19. Stealing from the spoils of war or damaged property.

20. Stealing from people, shops and other places.

21. Robbery (in all forms or types).

22. Denying and lying about Allah (SWT) and His Messenger.

23. Bearing false witness for personal benefits.

24. Gambling (in all forms or types).

25. Being dishonest and devious.

26. Speaking behind people's backs (backbiting).

27. Giving incorrect and wrongful oath.

28. Obtaining money through fraud or deception.

29. Running away from the battlefield and betrayal.

30. A leader deceiving his people and being unjust to them.

31. Giving and accepting bribes (all sorts of corruption).

32. Frequently or constantly lying and misleading people.

33. Being cruel and unkind to people and animals.

34. Betrayal of trust, spreading rumours and accusing people.

35. Women imitating men and men imitating women.

36. Spying for the enemy of the Muslims.

37. Deliberately giving short weights or measures for profit.

38. Selling wrong goods and deceiving customers.

39. Listening to vulgar music and watching TV programs, which will encourage anti-Islamic and sinful behaviour or acts.

40. Taking any kind of drugs (through any means).

41. Blasphemy against the Quran or Prophet Muhammad (pbuh) is strictly prohibited and regarded as an unforgivable crime. Whoever commits such a disgraceful act will be eligible for severe punishment in accordance with the Islamic laws.

42. Consulting or seeking help from 'spiritual healers' or 'fortune-tellers' and asking them to predict about their future through palm reading, numerology, astrological and any other means is forbidden in Islam. If anyone follows or practices these acts then this is regarded as contradiction to one of the Muslims belief that only Almighty Allah knows about our future deeds.

In the Sahih Al-Bukhari, the following sins are classified as major, and every Muslim must do their best to avoid them:

"Major sins, which Allah (SWT) most dislikes are:
- to associate another with Allah (SWT).
- to murder or killing of innocent people.
- to commit suicide and to swear to lie.
- disobedience to your father and mother."

Appendix F
Common misconceptions about Islam and Muslims perspective

Unfortunately, Islam is regarded and widely perceived to be rigid, prejudiced and the most misunderstood religion in the world, despite the fact that about 1.5 billion Muslims follow Islam, and reported to be the fastest growing faith in the world. Why is the most talked about and popular belief, which preaches peace, tolerance and harmony messages to all humanity (regardless of their colour, creed or gender), misinterpreted and unjustly portrayed in the media as being the intolerant, violent and unfriendly religion?

In this section, the author identifies and clarifies some of the most common myths buzzing around the world, and presents a true Islamic perspective with the aid of the relevant issue and verses as mentioned in the Quran. In order to promote love and peace among all communities and discard any misapprehension about Islam and its followers, it is essential that all readers do their level best to understand Islamic ideology, and promote much needed peace, mutual respect and tolerance in the present volatile world.

The following is a list of widespread and major misconceptions about Islam, which are currently perceived in the global media and public's minds. Islamic views are also briefly explained alongside for better understanding of the Muslim faith and its ethics:

Misconception No.1: 'Muslims are violent and terrorists'

Islamic viewpoint: This is the most common myth about Muslims advocated in the media by the anti-Islamic critics. It is often stated that 'All Muslims are not terrorist, but all terrorists are Muslims'. This illogical and prejudiced view promotes animosity, mistrust and backlash. If you conduct further search, then you will find that terrorists do not belong to one faith, race or region, and are spread across the world in many other religions such as Christianity,

Judaism and Hinduism, etc. Adherents of these faiths pursue their respective extremist ideologies for their causes and execute them without any mercy. Islam together with other major religions strongly condemns terrorising and killing of innocent people. It is worth restating that current political and territorial conflicts and oppressions of Muslims around the world generate frustration and hatred. As a result, a tiny minority of radical groups and young misled and vulnerable men unilaterally decide to take revenge against the aggressor. In the following surah, Allah (SWT) says that:

"Fight in the cause of Allah against those who fight against you, but begin not hostilities. Allah does not love aggressors."
(Ref: Al Quran - Surah Baqara C2:V190)

Misconception No.2: 'Islam oppresses and degrades women'

Islamic viewpoint: This is another unfounded and stereotyped perception about women instigated by Western society and critics. Where people think that a Muslim woman's role is limited to 'house work' only, and she is not allowed to express her feelings and statutory rights. This view about Muslim women is incorrect and based on ignorance. In fact, in Islam male and female are equal and there is no difference in gender duties. In most cases Muslim women play important and multiple roles as a daughter, a sister, a wife, a partner in income and a mother bringing up her children according to Islamic teachings, and this unique ability raises their respect and status in society. In addition, in Islamic history, women have played a very prominent role in every field, and in this regard, Prophet Muhammad's (pbuh) wife (Bibi Ayesha) and daughter's (Bibi Fatima) names are top of the list and well respected. In the following surahs, Allah (SWT) states that:

"They (women) are garments for you while you (men) are garments for them." (Ref: Al Quran - Surah Al Baqara C2:V187)

"Men are the protectors and maintainers of women, because Allah has given the one more (strength) than the other..." (Ref: C4:V34)

Misconception No.3: 'The Hajab or veil is suppressive'

Islamic viewpoint: Is vulgarity, dressing indecently and showing off the body permissible in any religion or society? In Islam, women are instructed to cover themselves adequately so that unrelated males are not encouraged or provoked and their evil thoughts are suppressed. The Hajab is certainly not oppressive; it is an obligatory duty, a personal choice and there is no compulsion. As long as women follow the Islamic ethics and dress code, and restrain themselves from wearing transparent clothes and excessive makeup. In the following surah, Allah (SWT) says about Hajab that:

"And say to the believing women that they should lower their gaze and guard their modesty; that they should not display their beauty and ornaments..."
(Ref: Al Quran - Surah An Noor C24:V31)

Misconception No.4: 'Islam was spread by the sword'

Islamic viewpoint: Again, this is not true - it is a myth and a pessimistic view of Islam portrayed by anti-Muslim agents in the global media. In fact, Islam is a peaceful and kind religion for all humanity, as it was spread through love, persuasion and without force. In the following surah, Allah (SWT) clearly states that:

"There is no compulsion in religion (Islam)..."
(Ref: Al Quran - Surah Baqara C2:V256)

Misconception No.5: 'Islam permits terrorism'

Islamic viewpoint: Islam certainly does not promote or allow terrorism. In fact, it is ignorance; poverty, territorial conflicts and injustice encourage terrorism and radicalisation. As a result, a few young misguided people behave foolishly to seek publicity. In addition, anti-Islamic critics frequently issue offensive statements, which instigate resentment. It must be re-stressed that vast majority of Muslims are peace loving and do not support terrorism.

Misconception No.6: 'Islam promotes suicide killings'

Islamic viewpoint: This is certainly untrue, as Islam opposes suicide attacks and killing of innocent people by either Muslims or non-Muslims anywhere in the world. Any person who acts rashly is misled and will be accountable to Allah for this awful act on the final judgment day. In the following surahs, Allah (SWT) says that:

"... and do not kill yourselves (nor kill one another)..."
(Ref: Al Quran - Surah An Nisa C4:V29)

"If anyone killed a person, unless it was for murder or spreading mischief on earth, it would be as if he killed all of mankind. And if anyone saved a life, it would be as if he had saved the lives of all mankind." (Ref: Surah Al Maida C5:V32)

Misconception No.7: 'All Muslims are Arabs'

Islamic viewpoint: This is another misperception based on ignorance. The fact is there are about 1.5 billon Muslims in the world and about 20% are Arabs and live in the Middle East, while 30% live in the Indian subcontinent. The rest are spread across the world in 57 nations. Islam is the second largest religion and is the fastest growing faith in Europe and North America; interestingly, women make up a large proportion of converts to Islam, overtaking men by 3 to 1. This shows that Islam is not a strict or bad religion, as some people think, and does have positive attributes, which attract more non-believers to accept Muslim faith.

Misconception No.8: 'Muslims are barbaric and cruel'

Islamic viewpoint: This perception is untrue and based on speculations and isolated cases. The media some times portray Muslims as cruel. For example, the way animals are killed in the Islamic tradition for eating purposes, and the severe punishments imposed for committing serious crimes may have created a negative image in some people's minds about Islam and its cultures.

Misconception No.9: 'All Muslim men marry four wives'

Islamic viewpoint: It is certainly untrue that all Muslim men have four wives. In fact, Islam is the only religion that encourages one marriage, but in special circumstances a Muslim man can marry up to four wives on the condition that he will treat them justly and equally in every respect (i.e. financially, socially etc.). In the following surah, Allah (SWT) clarifies this myth and says that:

"... Marry women of your choice, Two or three or four; but if ye fear that ye shall not be able to deal justly (with them), then only marry one..." (Ref: Al Quran - Surah An Nisa C4:V3)

Misconception No.10: 'Capital punishment is harsh'

Islamic viewpoint: In order to protect society from criminals and anti-social elements, Islam has a strict code of practice to control serious crimes such as murder, rape and adultery, etc. In fact, in Muslim countries, where strict Islamic law is enforced, the crime rate is much lower than in Western states, and in such cases capital punishment act as a deterrent for other people.

Misconception No.11: 'Muslims worship Muhammad'

Islamic viewpoint: This myth is again untrue and based on ignorance. All Muslims sincerely and totally believe in one God and worship him only. Prophet Muhammad (pbuh) is the last and final messenger and this is the part of the first pillar of Islam.

"And your God is One God; there is no God but He, Most Gracious, Most Merciful" (Ref: Surah Al Baqara - C2:V163)

Misconception No.12: 'Circling the Kaaba is idol worship'

Islamic viewpoint: Muslims do not worship Kaaba, only one God (Allah), and circle seven times around the Kaaba as part of their religious duty (Tuwaf), and face its direction five times a day everyday in prayer, no matter where they are in the world.

Misconception No.13: 'Muslims do not believe in Jesus'

Islamic viewpoint: In Islam, Prophet Jesus (pbuh) is highly regarded as a messenger of Allah (SWT). All Muslims believe in Allah's prophets and accept Jesus (pbuh) was one of his messengers. The following surah verifies the Muslims' claim and states that:

Say: "We believe in Allah and in what has been revealed to us and what was revealed to Abraham, Isma'il, Isaac, Jacob, and the Tribes, and in (the Books) given to Moses, Jesus, and the prophets, from their Lord: We make no distinction between one and another among them..."
(Ref: Al Quran - Surah Al Imran C3:V84)

Misconception No.14: 'Darwin's theory of evolution'

Islamic viewpoint: Muslims do not accept this unproven theory, which Charles Darwin published in 1859 in his book *'On the Origin of Species'*. Darwin stated that populations evolve over the course of generations through a process of natural selection. This theory contradicts the Muslim belief that it is God (Allah), who created the universe, animals and human beings, including Adam and Eve.

"It is He (Allah) who has created man from water..."
(Ref: Al Quran - Surah Al Furqan C25:V54)

"And Allah has created every animal from water..."
(Ref: Al Quran - Surah An Noor C24:V45)

Misconception No.15: 'Big Bang theory'

Islamic viewpoint: This scientific theory is also controversial. In 1927 Belgian priest, Georges Lemaitre claimed that the universe began with the explosion of a primeval atom about 13.7 billion years ago. Later in 1929, Edwin Hubble followed this unproven work. Islam rejects this theory as the Quran states that:

"It is Allah, Who has created the heavens and the earth, and all between them, in six Days..." *(Ref: Surah As Sajdah C32:V4)*

Appendix G
Major signs before 'Judgment Day'

All Muslims believe that there is another life after death and on the 'Judgment Day', all human beings' good and bad deeds will be accountable and rewarded accordingly. The following quotes from the Quran states what will happen on the final day:

"Every soul shall have a taste of death: and only on the Day of Judgment shall you be paid your full rewards..."
(Ref: Surah Al Imran - C3:V185)

"Surely, knowledge of the Hour is with Allah alone..."
(Ref: Surah Luqman - C31:V34)

"The trumpet shall be sounded, when behold! from the sepulchers (men) will rush forth to their Lord!"
(Ref: Surah Yaseen - C36:V51)

"It will be no more than a single blast, when lo! They will all be brought up before Us."
(Ref: Surah Yaseen - C36:V53)

"When the earth shall be shaken to its depths,"
(Ref:Surah Al Waqia - C56:V4)

"And the mountains shall be crumbled to atoms/dust,"
(Ref: Surah Al Waqia - C56:V5)

In this section, the author lists some of the major signs before the final day as stated in the Quran and hadith. The following signs will happen at different times and order before 'Judgment Day'.

- Knowledge of Islam will diminish and be taken away while ignorance will increase. People will not read the Quran.
- Wine (alcohol) will be drunk in vast quantities.

- Vulgarity and nudity will be more apparent.
- Earthquakes and cyclones will be more frequent, and there will be multiple deaths. (This is happening now).
- Bloodshed and killings will increase (i.e. wars, etc.)
- People will be more dishonest and untrustworthy.
- People will gather for prayer, but will be unable to find an Imam to lead them.
- The number of men will decrease, whilst the number of women will increase, until for every man there are fifty women.
- Muslims will take-over Rome.
- The Mahdi (guided one) will appear, and be the Imam of the Muslims.
- Jesus Christ (Prophet Issa (pbuh) will descend in Damascus, and pray behind the Mahdi.
- The anti-Christ (al-masih al-dajjal, the false Christ) will appear and 70,000 Jews will follow him from Isfahan (Iran).
- The Ya'jus and Ma'jus (Gog and Magog) will appear and cause problems. They will kill people.
- Prophet Issa (Jesus) will kill the anti - Christ.
- There will be so much wealth that it will be difficult to find someone to accept the charity.
- An Abyssinian leader with thin shins will destroy the Kaaba in Saudi Arabia.
- The sun will rise from the west instead of east.
- There will be no one left on the earth saying 'Allah'
- The Angel Israfeel will blow the trumpet and everyone will faint except as Allah wills.
- After the blow of the second trumpet, everyone will be resurrected and accountable for their deeds.

Appendix H
Islamic history (545 CE - 1948 CE)

The following is a summary of the important events listed in chronological order relating to Islamic history since 545 CE.

545 CE - Birth of Hazrat Abdullah (pbuh), the holy Prophet Muhammad's father.

570 CE - Birth of last Prophet Muhammad (pbuh).

577 CE - Prophet Muhammad (pbuh) visits Madina and the death of his mother Bibi Amina.

580 CE - Death of Hazrat Abdul Muttalib (pbuh), the grandfather of the holy Prophet Muhammad (pbuh).

583 CE - Prophet Muhammad's journey to Syria in the company of his uncle (Hazrat Abu Talib (pbuh) and meeting with priest Bahira, who predicted his prophethood.

595 CE - Prophet Muhammad (pbuh) married Bibi Khadija

610 CE - The first revelation in the cave Hira. The holy Prophet was selected as the messenger of God (Allah).

614 CE - Invitation to the Hashimites to accept Islam.

619 CE - Hazrat Abu Talib (pbuh) and Bibi Khadija died.

622 CE - Prophet Muhammad (pbuh) migrated to Madina.

624 CE - Battle of Badr. Expulsion of Jews from Madina.

625 CE - Battle of Uhad. Massacre of 70 Muslims at Bir Manna.

629 CE - Prophet Muhammad performed pilgrimage at Mecca.

630 CE - Conquest of Mecca. Battles of Hunsin, Auras and Taif.

632 CE - Prophet Muhammad (pbuh) performed Hajj.

632 CE - Prophet Muhammad (pbuh) passed away peacefully.

632 CE - Hazrat Abu Bakar (pbuh) was elected as the first Caliph.

634 CE - Hazrat Abu Bakr (pbuh) passed away peacefully and Hazrat Umar Farooq was elected as the second Caliph.

644 CE - Hazrat Othman/Usman was elected as the third Caliph.

656 CE - Hazrat Ali (pbuh) became the fourth Caliph.

661 CE - Hazrat Ali (pbuh) murdered while he was praying.

680 CE - Hazrat Hussain (pbuh) was killed at Karbala.

711 CE - Muslims advanced and conquered Spain.

1087 CE - Salah - ud Din captured Jerusalem from Christians.

1099 CE - The crusaders captured Jerusalem.

1245 CE - Muslims conquered Jerusalem.

1526 CE - Mughal emperor Babur conquered India.

1550 CE - Islam spread to Java, Moluccas and Burneo.

1605 CE - Mughal emperor Akbar died.

1627 CE - Mughal emperor Jahangir died.

1658 CE - Mughal emperor Shahjhan was removed.

1707 CE - Mughal emperor Aurangzeb passed away.

1712 CE - Mughal emperor Bahadur Shah Zafar died.

1813 CE - Mecca and Taif captured by Egyptian forces.

1828 CE - Russia declared war against Turkey.

1895 CE - Mirza Gulham Ahmad of Qadian proclaimed prophet hood and started the Ahmadia movement (sect) in India.

1947 CE - Creation of Pakistan from the Muslim majority area in India. Independence of Pakistan on 14th August 1947.

1948 CE - British relinquished their mandate over Palestine and on 14th May 1948 the state of Israel was created.

Appendix I
Photographs - Some of the most famous and holy mosques in the world

In Islam, all mosques are respectful and holy for Muslims, but the two most famous and holy mosques are located in Mecca and Madina (Saudi Arabia), and are very special. It is the wish of every Muslim to visit and pray there once in their lifetime. May Allah (SWT) fulfil their desire and allow them to pray there - Ameen!

The following photographs are in the public domain and show a glimpse of the most renowned and holy mosques in the world:

Bird's-eye view of the grand Mosque in Mecca

Kaaba in Mosque Harum Shareef - Mecca

Close up of Kaaba

The following photographs show the Prophet's mosque in the holy city of Madina (SA). As the final resting place of the last Prophet Muhammad and two caliphs (Hazrat Abu Bakr and Hazrat Umar (pbut), it is regarded the second largest and most holy site in Islam. The newly renovated mosque can now accomodate over one million worshippers during the Ramadan and Hajj pilgrimage.

Musjadi Nabvi - Prophet Muhammad's mosque in Madina (night view)

Bird's-eye view of the grand Musjadi Nabvi in Madina

The following photographs show other prominent holy mosques including the third most sacred mosque in Jeruslum, Madina, etc.

Masjid Quba - the first mosque in the history of Islam

Masjid Qiblatain in Madina

Al Aqsa Mosque in Jerusalem

17th century Blue Mosque in Turkey

Badshai mosque in Lahore Pakistan built during 1674

Jama Musjad in Delhi built by emperor Shahjhan

References and Abbreviations

Source of Information

- The holy Quran in Arabic, Urdu and English translations (Maulana Syed Shabbir Ahmed, Maulana Madudi, Abdullah Yusuf Ali and Mohammad Marmaduke Pickthall).
- Hadiths/Hadees (Sahih Al Bukhari and Sahih Al Muslim).
- Study of the Britannica, Encarta and Grolier encyclopaedias, Islamic history books and various agencies data i.e. US Bureau of Census, CIA Factbook, WRI, UN data and Pew Forum - US.
- The author's extensive study of the Quran and his analysis of each surah and ayah, which enabled him to write this unique guidebook with authentic quotes from the Quran and hadith. This will help to enhance the readers' knowledge.

Abbreviations

pbuh   peace be upon him (this abbreviation is used to bless all prophets and is an obligatory duty for Muslims).

SWT   Subhanahu Wa Ta'ala is a phrase used after Allah's name and praises his supremacy.

S   Surah (an Arabic word used instead of chapter).

C   Chapter (an English word used instead of surah).

V   Verse (an English word used instead of ayah).

Additional Comments

In order to avoid any misunderstanding, the author has excluded controversial, speculative and unsubstantiated issues in this book. He has focused his attention on the important historical facts, beliefs and pillars of Islam, the essence of the Quran and the mandatory duties that Allah (SWT) has conveyed and expects from every Muslim. The author has included relevant quotations in English translation as stated in the Quran and authentic hadith.

The author believes that it is the duty of all Muslims to endorse Allah's (SWT) messages in a true light, as he instructed through his book (the holy Quran). It is, therefore, requested that the constructive attributes of Islam (i.e. love, peace, unity and tolerance, etc.) are passed on to all human beings regardless of their religion or race. This would be the most significant contribution one could make in one's lifetime and Allah (SWT) will reward accordingly.

This book is a voluntary work and the author has dedicated all his contribution to Allah and humanity for promoting Islam through Dawah (invitation) without any personal or financial motives. It is worth stating that the author does not represent any religious or political party, as over 90% of the contents of this book are authentic and based on his in-depth study of the Quran and Sunnah (Hadith). However, the analysis expressed between pages 63 and 67 are the author's personal views based on his observations and experience.

The following messages of last and final Prophet Muhammad (pbuh) (as narrated in the Sahih Al-Bukhari and Sahih Al-Muslim) emphasise the importance of learning, sharing knowledge and propagating Islam through Dawah as part of Islamic teaching and the obligatory duty of every Muslim.

"The ink of the scholar is more righteous (holy) than the blood of the martyr."

"Seek knowledge from the cradle to the grave."

"One learned man is harder on the devil than a thousand of ignorant worshippers."

This book is part of a non-profitable project for humanity, and all sale proceeds will be donated to poor and needy people (i.e. orphans, widows, sick children, OAP, the terminally ill and cancer patients, etc.) through ZAK Trust (UK) and other reputable charities.

The author would welcome any constructive feedback and valuable suggestions, and can be contacted via e: **makCEng@hotmail.co.uk**

Acknowledgements

I would like to thank all my family members for their love, respect and full co-operation, and their commitment to keep the family's traditions and values intact in the future. I, therefore, would like to extend my gratitude and list names of my senior and junior family members as a token of appreciation, and I sincerely thank them for their unconditional love and respect they have given to me:

- Late (R) Army Contractor - Ch. Gulham Rasool Khan.
- Late (R) Army Contractor - Ch. Sardar Khan.
- Late (R) Editor Pakistan Times - Mohammad Aslam Khan.
- Late Afzal Khan and his sons Air Commodore (Pakistan Air Force) Akmal Khan and Squadron Leader (PAF) Dr Tafazal Khan.
- Late (R) Advocate and Police Superintendent - Dalawer Khan Awan.
- Late Engr Zakria Khan Awan and his sons Kibria and Yahya Khan Awan.
- Late Engr Nusrullah Khan Awan and his son Naeem Khan Awan.
- Asad Khan, Mona, Umara, Zara, Rehan and Imran.
- Silman Nomani, Munaza, Sumaira, Ayesha and Farhan.
- Late Dr Khawar Tauheed and his family Suhaila, Subhan and Zoona.
- Late (R) Professor Dr Abu Bakar (University of the Punjab) and his sons Yasir, Uzair, Saria and Usama Abu Bakar.
- Nusrat Khan.
- Anwar Khan.
- My wife Najma and her siblings.

In addition, I would like to thank Professor Dr Akbar Ahmed for his support, valuable comments and positive contribution, which encouraged me even more to continue my mission and propagate authentic teachings of Islam to diverse faiths and communities.

Index

Islam is a peaceful religion and promotes love, peace, mutual respect, religious and social tolerance among all diverse cultures.

It is obligatory for Muslims to respect other prominent prophets like Abraham, Moses and Jesus, etc.

Islam Prohibits:

- Denying God's (Allah's) existence
- Creating associates of the one and only God
- Disregarding the pillars and beliefs of Islam
- Blasphemy against the Quran and Prophet Muhammad (pbuh)
- Suicide attacks and killing of innocent people
- Terrorising and kidnapping people
- Forced marriages and oppressing women
- Stealing or committing other crimes
- Polygamy, adultery, drinking alcohol and taking any kind of drugs
- Cruelty to human beings and animals
- Dishonesty, backbiting and nudity
- Performing black magic and misleading people
- Disobeying and neglecting parents, etc...

DID YOU KNOW ?

According to Muslims faith, Islam
was first brought to earth by Prophet Adam
(pbuh), and subsequently about 124,000
prophets preached the message of one and only
true deity (Almighty God). This message was
later conveyed to different tribes and nations
through various prophets (i.e. Nuh, Abraham,
Moses, Jesus, etc.). However, between 610 CE
and 632 CE the last and final Prophet
Muhammad (pbuh) completed the religion of
Islam for humanity through the revelation of the
holy Quran. (Source: Al Quran and Hadith)

In the Quran, it is stated that:

*"Behold, thy Lord said to the angels: I will create a
vicegerent on earth…" "And He taught Adam the
nature of all things…"*
(Source: Surah Baqara C2: V30 and V31)

*"… This day have I perfected your religion for you
and completed my favour unto you and have chosen
for you a religion Al ISLAM…"*
(Source: Surah Al Maidah C5: V3)

Muslim population in the world

A report published by the Pew Forum on Religion and Public Life (US) in 2009 with census data from 232 countries and territories presented the following key features about Muslim population across the globe:

- There are 1.57 billion Muslims populate the World
- Of the total Muslim population, 10 - 13% are Shia Muslims and 87 - 90% are Sunni Muslims
- There are currently 2.1 billion Christians, 900 million Hindus, 14 million Jews and 1.1 billion Atheists worldwide
- 61.9% Muslims live in the Asia and Pacific region
- 20.1% Muslims live in the Middle East and North Africa
- 15.3% Muslims reside in Sub-Saharan Africa
- 2.4% Muslims live in Europe
- 0.3% Muslims live in North America.

Muslim population by geographical location and region - 2009

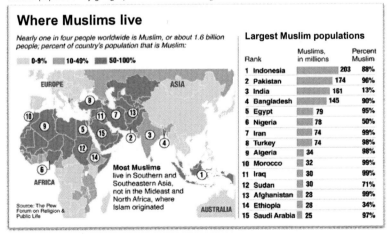

Where Muslims live

Nearly one in four people worldwide is Muslim, or about 1.6 billion people; percent of country's population that is Muslim:

0-9%   10-49%   50-100%

Most Muslims live in Southern and Southeastern Asia, not in the Mideast and North Africa, where Islam originated

Source: The Pew Forum on Religion & Public Life

Largest Muslim populations

Rank		Muslims, in millions	Percent Muslim
1	Indonesia	203	88%
2	Pakistan	174	96%
3	India	161	13%
4	Bangladesh	145	90%
5	Egypt	79	95%
6	Nigeria	78	50%
7	Iran	74	99%
8	Turkey	74	98%
9	Algeria	34	98%
10	Morocco	32	99%
11	Iraq	30	99%
12	Sudan	30	71%
13	Afghanistan	28	99%
14	Ethiopia	28	34%
15	Saudi Arabia	25	97%

In 1927, Belgian priest, Georges Lemaitre claimed that the universe began with the explosion of a primeval atom about 13.7 billion years ago. In 1862, the physicist William Thomson of UK published calculations that fixed the age of earth at between 20 million and 400 million years. Later in 1953, Clair Patterson of US calculated an age of earth about 4.55 billion years. This has remained unchanged for 50 years. It is also estimated that life on earth existed between 10 and 20 million years ago.

(Source: Britannica 2005 and Wikipedia)

The Quran revealed over 1400 years ago that:

"It is Allah who has created the heavens and the earth, and all between them, in six days…"
(Source: Surah As Sajdah C32: V4)

"Man We did create from a quintessence (of clay)"
(Source: Surah Al Mominoon C23: V12)

"It is Allah Who alternates the Night and the Day..."
(Source: Surah An Noor C24: V44)

Demographic status of Islam and major religions

The author presents a brief statistical analysis, and projected population growth of Islam and other major religions, and how the trends are likely to develop during the next few decades. In order to preserve enduring peace in the world, it is essential that we all try to understand diverse faiths and cultures.

- In 2007, CNN News reported that about 6 million Muslims live in America, and 25% (1.5 million) have converted to Islam after the 9/11 incident.

- In 2008, NBC News televised that every year about 20,000 people accepts Islam in US, and about 66% are women.

- It is estimated from the data issued by the World Research Institute (WRI) - US that by 2050, the world's birth rate will drop about 25% and fatality rate will increase by 7%.

- It is projected that by 2050, world population will increase to 9.3 billion. Muslims will represent about 2.5 billion. Source: UN and US Bureau of Census, 2008

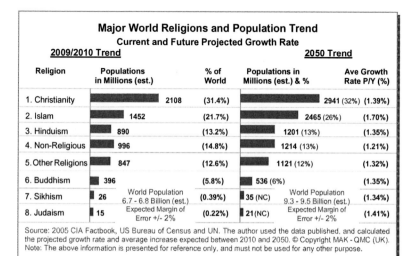

Major World Religions and Population Trend
Current and Future Projected Growth Rate

| Religion | 2009/2010 Trend | | 2050 Trend | |
	Populations in Millions (est.)	% of World	Populations in Millions (est.) & %	Ave Growth Rate P/Y (%)
1. Christianity	2108	(31.4%)	2941 (32%)	(1.39%)
2. Islam	1452	(21.7%)	2465 (26%)	(1.70%)
3. Hinduism	890	(13.2%)	1201 (13%)	(1.35%)
4. Non-Religious	996	(14.8%)	1214 (13%)	(1.21%)
5. Other Religions	847	(12.6%)	1121 (12%)	(1.32%)
6. Buddhism	396	(5.8%)	536 (6%)	(1.35%)
7. Sikhism	26 World Population 6.7 - 6.8 Billion (est.)	(0.39%)	35 (NC) World Population 9.3 - 9.5 Billion (est.)	(1.34%)
8. Judaism	15 Expected Margin of Error +/- 2%	(0.22%)	21 (NC) Expected Margin of Error +/- 2%	(1.41%)

Source: 2005 CIA Factbook, US Bureau of Census and UN. The author used the data published, and calculated the projected growth rate and average increase expected between 2010 and 2050. © Copyright MAK - QMC (UK). Note: The above information is presented for reference only, and must not be used for any other purpose.

DID YOU KNOW ?

- **Islam** - was completed by the last Prophet Muhammad (pbuh) between 610 CE and 632 CE through the revelation of the holy Quran in Mecca and Madina (Saudi Arabia).

- **Judaism** - is one of the first known monotheistic (Abrahamic) religions emerged between 2000 and 1500 BCE through Moses.

- **Hinduism** - emerged during 1500 - 500 BCE with no single founder or religious authorty.

- **Buddaism** - introduced by Gautama Buddah during 500 BCE.

- **Christianity** - descended from Judaism between 6 BCE and 30 CE - (Prophet Jesus).

- **Sikhism** - introduced by Guru Nanak Dev during 1500 CE in India.

- **Communism** - started during the 19th and 20th centuries in the Soviet Union and China.

- The majority of other religions emerged during the last 1000 years or so ago.

(Source: Britannica 2005 and BBC Religion)

Author's 5R Messages

Read	**Refine**	**Re-educate**
the Quran with meanings and act upon its messages	your knowledge and share with other communities	your family, friends and other people about ISLAM

Respect	**Reject**
other peoples religion, beliefs and their views	and do not support or follow radical and biased ideologies

General Notes

Islam promotes integrity, unity, acquiring and sharing knowledge, kindness, equality and justice for all civilization without any compulsion or discrimination.

The author hopes that his contribution will encourage more interaction, interfaith dialogue, mutual respect and social cohesion among all communities.

The author also takes this opportunity and thank all learned readers for their anticipated co-operation and efforts to make this world more peaceful for humanity and our future generations.

Islam is for all human beings

"...Our Lord, do not take us to task if we forget or make mistakes. Our Lord, do not burden us as You burdened those before us. Our Lord, do not burden us with more than we have strength to bear. Parden us, forgive us, and have mercy on us. You are our Protector, so help us against evil spirit."

(Reference: Al Quran, Surah Baqara C2: V286)